The **END** *from the*
BEGINNING

The End from the Beginning

The END *from the* BEGINNING

Kristin Hardiman

Remember the former things,

those of long ago;

I am God, and there is no other;

I am God, and there is none like me.

I make known

the end from the beginning,

from ancient times,

what is still to come.

*I say, **"My purpose will stand."***

- Isaiah 46:9-10

SPECIAL THANKS

I just want to thank my mother, Brenda Hall, for never giving up on me, even when I gave up on myself. Thank you for loving me unconditionally, even when I broke your heart and made terrible life decisions — all the while you were on your knees praying for me. You taught us biblical principles as children, and would often quote Proverbs 22:6, *"Train up a child in the way he should go and when he is old he will not depart from it."* Seeing you push through years of trials and tribulations and overcome by God's grace, I now know the strength you drew from was your Jesus. Now I truly know this Jesus, seeing your faith and standing on the promises of God. You sacrificed your entire life to take care of your four girls as a single mother. You always put God first, then us. There was not a day that went by when you didn't show us we were loved. We were always a team. You stood right beside us, even in the darkness, holding our hand and holding the hand of God, praying us into the light. When I could finally see, I saw the Mighty Woman of God that you are, Mom. Thank you for the example you set for me. I would not be the woman of God I am today if it were not for you. Love you, Mom!

I also want to thank every one of my sisters — Ashley, Erica, Bre and Kalie — for the close relationship we all have. We have been through so much together and have had a lot of the same struggles. I am proud of each of you. I hope this book inspires you and I hope I have been and have set the example God had in mind. The hand of God is on our lives and I know we will all rise to the high calling that was placed upon us before the foundations of the earth were formed. I believe our ministry is together and will soon come to pass. I love you with all my heart!

Your big sister, Kristin

In addition, I thank all of my friends and family for your support!

A very special thanks to my great-grandmother, Blanche Jones, who prayed for me under the blackberry tree. Two generations prior to me and my sisters walking into salvation, the Lord met my grandmother in that secret place where she prayed — under the blackberry tree. She prayed for me before I was even born and the Lord answered her. My sisters were at the altar and the Lord gave our pastor a word of knowledge that no one could have known but God. He said to them, "You guys had a grandmother who used to pray in this certain spot. Those prayers have been placed in a bottle on a shelf.

Right now God is pulling those payers off the shelf, out of those bottles and you and your family's salvation is a result of those answered prayers." At that time we had no idea of any certain spot or any blackberry tree. I was still in darkness but my sisters began to come forth and the Lord said to them, "The prayers that our grandmother prayed were being pulled out of a bottle in heaven and were being released." Her prayer was for us to come into salvation. That was why we were radically saved. The testimony in this book is an answered prayer. We then went to our grandma, Alma Jones, and asked her if she knew anything about a blackberry tree. She paused for a moment and shockingly said, "Oh, my God! Your great-grandmother was a prayer warrior, and she prayed under the blackberry tree on the hill early in the mornings." That was a sign from God only He could know. He is faithful from generation to generation and His Word says (Revelation 5:8), "*And when he had taken it, the four living creatures and the 24 elders fell down before the lamb. Each one had a harp and they were holding golden bowls full of incense, which are the prayers of God's people.*" Only He can know the end from the beginning, and only He can take a moment from two generations past and make it known in the present.

I love you, Grandma Blanche Jones!

DEDICATION

This book
is dedicated to
Alice Gates,
my biggest fan!
She wanted her ceiling
to be my floor.

CONTENTS

PREFACE

A young woman walks into the church service very timidly and almost awkwardly.

I see her looking around and she walks up to me before the service. She may have attended one of our services, but this time she comes directly to me right before we start.

She says to me: "I heard you interpret dreams."

I respond: "Yes, prophetic dreams from the Lord."

During this time, around 2012 or so, I was teaching a prophetic series called "A Time of Visitation." The theme was centered around the fact that Jesus can visit you in dreams and visions.

In comes Kristin Hardiman, the young woman mentioned earlier (and this book's author). She had a dream and proceeded to tell me about it!

Jesus visited her in a dream and initiated one of the greatest testimonies of deliverance, healing and recovery that I've ever witnessed.

For years I've told the story of this young woman who had this visitation from Jesus in a dream. We lost contact for a few years — then seemingly out of nowhere I get a call from … Kristin Hardiman!

I was overwhelmed with excitement, and the testimony of her life since that encounter has been amazing.

Kristin has become like a spiritual daughter to me. Her life is a testimony to what the power of the gospel can do and the Life of the Spirit can produce.

God has called Kristin for such a time as this! Father uses her in prophetic dreams and has given her a passion for the lost, especially in the area of addiction. Kristin was delivered from addiction herself.

This book is one that should be read by everyone!

Kristin's life story will bring healing and deliverance to so many people. I'm excited to be associated with someone with such a powerful testimony and life.

– Apostle Chad Collins

INTRODUCTION

Every believer's life is a journey.

We want to welcome you to our dear friend Kristin Hardiman's journey from darkness to marvelous light, from a life of bondage to life of freedom in Christ Jesus. She has come from a total shipwrecked life to a life of blessing and prosperity. Because of her total commitment to Jesus Christ, we have personally witnessed a glorious transformation from a life of addictions.

She herself personally is the greatest testament to this book. Because of her transformation, many lives have and are being changed by the power of the Holy Spirit working in and through her life.

We believe that as you read this book, you can and will be changed by the Mighty Power of an Almighty God! We release God's blessings on all who read this book. May your life, and the life of others that you share her testimony with, be forever changed.

Working in the Master's Kingdom together!

- Kristin's Pastors, Ron and Christine Kissel

1

CHAPTER 1

A Dark Place

The end of my darkness in bondage, and the beginning of my new life in the light ...

My past is not who I am, but its trials have made me the woman of God I am today. I have overcome by the grace of God the sins and bondages that held me captive 35 of my 40 years on this earth.

I found my Savior Jesus Christ in the deepest and darkest place I have ever been — overwhelmed in addiction, on my way to an eternity called hell.

I had just overdosed on heroin and was unconscious. My respiratory system had shut down for three hours.

All I can remember is my vision slowly grew very dim. I knew I was going to need help because I couldn't speak. I intended to crawl to the couch where Brandi was so she would recognize I needed help, but I passed out and fell to the floor instead.

I clearly remember I looked up and saw the earth. I felt as if I was under the earth and all the people in it. I felt as if I was under the earth and looking through glass. I knew immediately I had died. I was trying to wrap my mind around what was occurring, trying to receive the thought. I couldn't even tell my mom and my sisters I needed help. I was surrounded by what seemed like millions of people who were in this uncomfortable almost suffocating place under the earth.

I was then drawn into another realm. The vision I had was me lying completely naked like a child in my Father's arms. Jesus was holding my lifeless body in His arms. I felt His love. My eyes were closed but I could see everything around me. He was standing before the throne of God. I saw and felt the light and glory of God the Father — immeasurable, boundless, brighter than anything I had ever seen! Jesus was interceding for me. He spoke a word: "She loves me."

Suddenly he put His lips to mine and blew life into me. I was resurrected. I suddenly woke up in my apartment lying on my bed gasping for air. I was now alive and conscious.

My friend, Jon, and his mother had been trying to revive me for three hours. I remember sitting on the side of my bed. By the way everyone was looking at me I knew something was seriously wrong with me. I could just feel this heaviness in the atmosphere.

I remember asking them, "Can I walk?" I felt like if I got up and started walking everyone would know that I was okay.

At that moment I had converted back into a child. Brandi told me: "Give her a hug," speaking of Jon's mother who was standing directly in front of me. She had been in the room for the past three hours of what was probably a nightmare for them, but divine intervention for me.

I was living in sin and had made a decision between Brandi and God. I chose her. I turned my back on Him for the last time. I ignored every warning He had given me, every dream, every word that I knew in my heart was the truth. I had fallen to a point of no return. I have never known a darker place and have seen many dark days and years, but the power of darkness had taken over my mind completely. I was facing eternity, helpless, hopeless. My time on earth was up. Hell was waiting for me. The angel of death was in position to take my soul. If I was able to cry out no one could hear me. I was in a realm no man can reach. I had rejected Jesus my entire life and refused to serve Him. Then here came my

Father, my Savior Jesus Christ in His infinite glory and unfailing love I did not deserve.

Why?

I'll never know until the day we meet. The only thing I am certain of is, He loves me. I was put back on this earth alive.

So, I was able to comprehend what she said. I stood up and wrapped my arms around her neck in the pure innocence of a child. She was speechless and in awe. They had just witnessed a miracle. They left and went back upstairs. I spent the rest of my night in a daze, slowly coming back to myself, still catching my breath from the experience I had been through unknowingly. I was just in the presence of God.

Being in the presence of God will change you forever and, in that moment, I was forever changed.

Over the next couple of weeks, I started asking questions trying to put the pieces back together. Brandi told me she saw a dark cloud over me while I was unconscious. I know now that was the angel of death coming to take my soul.

She said, "Then the dark cloud that was hovering over you disappeared."

Clearly my Savior came and saved me from the power of darkness.

Brandi was the woman I fell in love with when I was in rehab in Hotel Louisville. I started dating her while I was in the program. She was just as broken and confused as I was. She was dealing with a lot of pain from her failed marriage and losing custody of her children while in addiction. We dated the whole time I was in the program. It was great in the beginning. We were in love. She was still married, but she and her husband were separated.

That was the story of my life. I'd always seem to get myself caught up in adultery. I had never had the intention of being involved with a married woman, a trap the enemy has set for me on more than one occasion. I fell for it every single God-forsaken time. I was just looking for what everyone else seemed to be looking for — someone to love me, someone to tell me I'm beautiful, someone to be waiting for me every day when I get off work, someone to wake up and kiss every morning before I start my day. I was blinded and deceived by darkness.

Sin always has a way of disguising itself, making itself look a lot like love, when really it's lust — a lie covered in outward beauty straight from the pit of hell, just waiting for you to fall in. Sent by the devil and his angels to kill, steal and destroy everything in you that is good, everything God has blessed you with. To steal any joy you may have, what little faith you are still able to hold on to, what little peace you have left in you, and all the hope you had just to get out of bed this morning

— hoping today would be a new day, with all the love you have in your heart, even though no one seems to love you back. It took all your strength to smile in the morning, and by the end of the day depression had taken over and you felt even more worthless than you did yesterday.

So, you try to do anything to numb yourself from the pain and brokenness you feel. Time to drink, time to get high. And you find yourself in a bottomless pit of guilt, shame, and remorse. Again, story of my freakin' life. There is Satan at his finest, thinking he has won, leaving you on your knees, powerless.

Brandi's husband knew we were together. They had been separated for a while. That made it easier to justify our relationship. They were decided on divorce, but just didn't have it on paper. I knew better than that. I had been through this many times before, all ending broken-hearted and a pitiful disaster. I chose to listen to the wrong voice. The devil was telling me, "It's okay." The power of darkness, the power of that sin burning inside me, was louder than any other voice. All the while the Holy Spirit was whispering, "You have done this before. You have experienced the wrath from it time and time again. Do what you know is truth."

I walked in my fleshly desires and they won that battle, but not the fight.

Back to life with Brandi at my apartment, a small room I was renting out of a house, with four other rooms occupied by crack and heroin addicts in just as bad of shape as I was. We were all one big happy drug-addicted family. We shared drugs, food, ripped each other off when we were desperate, and still we would continue on like it never happened. I was at the lowest point I had ever been. I was shooting up heroin, smoking crack, and doing any and everything I could to get high. This was a deathtrap the enemy had set for me and I fell deep in it.

I was so in love with Brandi I was blinded. She was all that mattered to me. If she was happy, I was happy. If she wasn't happy, I was killing myself trying to make her happy. I didn't even go to visit my family. She had made me believe she was all that I needed and she was the only one who loved me. She was wrong.

My family still loved me and continued praying for me to come home. I was too ashamed to go. I didn't want them to see how bad I looked, and how far I had fallen. I didn't like myself, let alone love myself. I couldn't even look at myself in the mirror anymore. When I would take a shower and get dressed in the morning, I wouldn't dare look. I was afraid of what I was going to see. If I looked anything remotely close to what I felt like and took a look at the place I had brought myself to, I thought I would be better off dead.

I worked for a temporary service in Louisville that sent us out to different factories. They paid next to nothing, just enough to keep us from starving and barely enough to support our cigarette and drug addiction. Our rent was four months behind, and we were on the verge of being evicted.

There was something about Mrs. Jordan, our landlord. She was a successful black woman who knew the Lord and showed me mercy. She knew I was doing the best I could with what I had. I had made a great first impression. I was sober, just coming out of a halfway house. I was at Wayside prior to, and I did what I knew to do. I paid my first month's rent and deposit. I came to her in a professional manner, using proper language which I was taught by my mother.

My intentions were good and, even then, the grace of God was all over me. I rented the room and got everything together, thinking Brandi and I were going to live happily ever after. Boy, was I in for a surprise! The Holy Spirit had warned me while I was at Wayside that, if I went back into addiction, the devil was going to kill me. I knew it deep down in my heart this was truth.

The Holy Spirit also spoke to me and said, "You know, before this world ends or you die you have got to get your heart right with God."

I ignored that warning once again and continued to go on about what I was doing.

So, Brandi had been kicked out of rehab for the second time for relapsing, and I guess I really thought I was going to save her. I couldn't even save myself. Like my mother always said: "The blind leading the blind."

Ain't that the truth! That has become one of the realest things I have ever known.

Brandi called me a week later, after she shacked up with some random guy for a week, asking to move in. I was just waiting for her to come back. She had no money, no place to stay, and had been high for a week. There I was with open arms, like I was saving someone. I was doing nothing more than getting myself in deeper and deeper. It was a trap, a setup. The devil had a master plan to take me out. He was going for the kill this time.

Brandi and I became closer, all a part of my plan to make her fall in love with me. I wanted to marry her and promised her I would take care of her. I did just that. I took as good care of her as I possibly could. I made sure she had everything she needed. I always made sure she ate good. I didn't care. I was thankful for everything I had. It didn't matter to me. I was very humbled and told myself, "If she is happy, I'm happy."

The truth is: There was nothing I could do to make her whole. She had lost everything. I poured all the love I had to give and then some. It still was never enough. I don't know how I managed, but I got up every morning at 4 a.m., walked 18 blocks to catch the city bus, and rode all the way across town — a 45-minute bus ride just to sign in at a temporary service that may or may not send me anywhere for the day. If I was lucky, I would work an 8-hour shift for most days at $7.25 an hour, sometimes $8 if I got sent to a decent place. It was only temporary. We would get paid cash every day.

After the temporary service took out their cut, including gas money, I would make a whopping $54 a day. I then cashed my check, hopped on the 45-minute bus ride home, picked up dinner for us (usually pizza and Mt. Dew), and walked 18 blocks home. And there she was, blowing me up all day, waiting impatiently for me just so I could go on another mission: a bag of dope. So, then I walk another 10-20 blocks to meet my dope dealer and get high. And we thought we were living the dream, doing the things adults do all night. Sleep and wake up and do it all over again.

A few months passed and I was now in debt, owing Mrs. Jordan past due rent. She was threatening to evict us if we didn't catch it up. I called my mom for $200 dollars one time, and she gave it to me. She usually sent me $40 every week, sometimes every two weeks, to help me out just like she had done while I was in rehab. Then she stopped. She wanted me to move back home.

About this time, Brandi and I argued every day. Our relationship had become even more toxic than it was before. She tore me down in every possible way she could. I was struggling in every area in my life, barely able to function. At this point I was using heroin every day. I had pushed my family away. It had been over a year since I had last seen my family. I was listening to Brandi and the enemy whispering lies into my mind. I knew all my sisters were sober and living for the Lord, so I believed they didn't want anything to do with me, which was a lie. I was so oblivious to the truth. I remembered what is was like to live for Jesus. I was so happy and full of joy. I knew I was a long way from that and very far away from God. I felt like I could never get back to that, like I had lost Him forever. The love of God seemed like a very distant memory. But He was still there, in the depths of my heart and soul. I was just waiting for death to roll up on me. What had I done?

The Lord had warned me. He came to visit me in my dreams numerous times. He gave me warning through people, through His Word, and the Holy Spirit. I ignored Him every time. I ran with Brandi as far as I could go away from Him. I felt like I had gone way too far this time. How could He ever forgive someone like me? I felt like I was beyond reconciliation on a highway to hell and there was no turning back. I just knew my time was almost up. I guessed I would just make the best of it. I believed I deserved all the misery I experienced day after day, and the mental abuse.

I felt my spirit being taken from me little by little. I had nothing left that was good in me, nothing to look forward to except getting high. I deserved everything I got. The love of God seemed like a very distant memory, far from reality.

I tried to read the Bible a few times while Brandi and I were arguing, trying to find my way back, trying to find some peace of mind. I was sick of feeling this way.

Nothing could suppress the pain anymore. I was tired. My mind was wearing down. My body was fatigued. My spirit was stolen. I couldn't even crack a smile. The Kristin I knew loved to smile. I had such a beautiful smile. The light of God used to radiate from me. How could this be? I was a child of the most-high God, now captured in Satan's dark dungeon — overwhelmed with the weights of sin, shackled in chains that were unbreakable. I thought I had a faith that was unshakable.

What happened to the God I knew, but chose not to serve? Where was the God who said He would never leave me or forsake me? I felt all alone, forsaken. My heart was broken. Where are You, God? Where are You when I need You the most? Where is this Savior everyone speaks of? I can't find You. Lord, show Your face. I need You!

No answer. I knew where my answer was. It was in the Word of God, the book I had gone to as a last resort over the years. Well, this was a last resort, and I was at the bottom of myself, out of drugs and alcohol. It's bad when you hurt and have nothing to numb yourself with. The pain was unbearable. I would pick up my Bible, wipe off the dust, and start reading it. I would get just one verse into it and Brandi would yell, "Stop reading that."

Now is not the time, I thought.

But now was the perfect time. I had to find some hope from somewhere. I hardly had the strength to carry on. I knew that was the devil speaking through her. He had me right where he wanted me. You're easy to take out when you are at your weakest point. I knew that the enemy was trying to steal the Word of God from me, just like he had stolen everything else. He had stolen my spirit, my innocence, my dignity, my self-worth and, most importantly, he had stolen my praise.

John 10:10-13 (NASB) says, *"The thief comes only to steal and kill and destroy. I came that they may have life, and have it abundantly. I am the good shepherd. The good shepherd lays down his life for the sheep. The hired hand, who is not the shepherd and does not own the sheep, sees the wolf coming and leaves the sheep and runs away — and the wolf snatches them and scatters them. The hired hand runs away because a hired hand does not care for the sheep."*

The wolf that snatches the sheep is Satan. But Jesus is the Good Shepherd.

Jesus says, *"I am the good shepherd. I know my own and my own know me, just as the Father knows me and I know the Father. And I lay down my life for the sheep* (John 10:10-13, NASB).

No matter what happens, the truth of the matter is I still belonged to God. I was a lost sheep and Jesus had already died for me.

THE END FROM THE BEGINNING

2

CHAPTER 2

Things Stolen

Satan had stolen the identity I had found in Christ Jesus at Hotel Louisville. I was introduced to the things of the Spirit for the first time in my life. God was visiting me in my dreams. He would often send me a word through Apostle Chad Collins. I found a higher, deeper, supernatural realm in Jesus Christ — the realest thing I have ever known. I had this freedom I had never walked in before. Then here came the enemy with the same old tricks. At that time I was diligently seeking God, fasting and praying. I was alive! My spirit had been dead but something in me awakened. Truth and life were being poured into my life, my soul, and my spirit.

But the flesh was weak. I had been feeding my flesh with the things of this world all my life. My flesh-man was still in control of my body. I was at war for my soul and didn't even realize how important it was for me to fight. So, this beautiful young woman made her way into my life, my heart, and my emotions. She told me everything I wanted to hear, gave me the attention I so desperately needed. I felt everything I had longed to feel. Lust and affection were the things my body craved. They were what the devil used to trap me every time. He told me a lie and I believed it.

Love was a word I knew not the real meaning. My entire life I had confused lust and love. Most people think the same exact thing. I thought I had fallen in love with Brandi, and obviously I thought she was in love with me. In reality, I believed a big fat lie! Lust is not love. I was too broken and weighed down in sin to receive a true revelation. True revelation only comes from God. Understanding also comes from God. You find those things in His word. I had been way too busy in life to read the Word and most certainly was not living by it. I knew bits and pieces of the Word, enough to know what I was doing was wrong, but didn't have enough strength, and no spiritual weapons, to fight with. My spirit and flesh were in a constant battle, and my flesh always won. But I'm still in the fight! I have the Victory!

3

CHAPTER 3

From The Beginning

Now from the beginning …

I was chosen by God before the foundations of the earth were formed. I was called to share the good news to the poor.

The prophet Isaiah said:

He has sent me to bring good news to the oppressed,
   to bind up the brokenhearted,
to proclaim liberty to the captives,
   and release to the prisoners;
to proclaim the year of the Lord's favor,
   and the day of vengeance of our God;

to comfort all who mourn;
to provide for those who mourn in Zion—
  to give them a garland instead of ashes,
the oil of gladness instead of mourning,
  the mantle of praise instead of a faint spirit.
They will be called oaks of righteousness,
  the planting of the Lord, to display his glory.
They shall build up the ancient ruins,
  they shall raise up the former devastations;
they shall repair the ruined cities,
  the devastations of many generations.
Strangers shall stand and feed your flocks,
  foreigners shall till your land and dress your vines;
but you shall be called priests of the Lord,
  you shall be named ministers of our God;
you shall enjoy the wealth of the nations,
  and in their riches you shall glory.
Because their shame was double,
  and dishonor was proclaimed as their lot,
therefore they shall possess a double portion;
  everlasting joy shall be theirs.
For I the Lord love justice,
  I hate robbery and wrongdoing;
I will faithfully give them their recompense,
  and I will make an everlasting covenant with them.
Their descendants shall be known among the nations,
  and their offspring among the peoples;

all who see them shall acknowledge
  that they are a people whom the Lord has blessed.
I will greatly rejoice in the Lord,
  my whole being shall exult in my God;
for he has clothed me with the garments of salvation,
  he has covered me with the robe of righteousness,
as a bridegroom decks himself with a garland,
  and as a bride adorns herself with her jewels.
For as the earth brings forth its shoots,
  and as a garden causes what is sown in it to spring up,
so the Lord God will cause righteousness and praise
  to spring up before all the nations.
(Isaiah 61:1b-11, NRSV)

The Lord made this covenant with me when He came down on a staircase from heaven, shaking His head telling me, "No!" — referring to the gay lifestyle I was in.

That was the one thing I did not want to let go of. I wanted Him to take everything else — the desire for drugs and alcohol that was killing me slowly. But I just didn't want to let go of the same-sex attraction I'd had my entire life.

When you see the face of the Lord, that is a covenant that, no matter how far you fall or how deep you go into the dark pit of Satan, He will deliver you for His glory. I'm so glad I saw the face of the Lord in that dream.

I grew up in Princeton, Indiana. My father was a farmer and my mother was in the administrative field at a power plant. I remember when I was around the age of 7 or 8, in the 3rd grade. Mrs. Inghuhn was my first-grade teacher and I just loved her daughter, Becky. For some odd reason I used to call her "Boy," referring to her as a tomboy like myself.

I played basketball. It was my escape and it was my passion. I was naturally good at it. I spent most of my time practicing. I was going to be the first woman in the NBA. I also played softball. I was naturally good at that as well, but my heart was all about basketball.

My home life consisted of my dad being full of anger towards my mother, but I loved my dad. I just hated the things he did, especially while he was drinking. At this age I remember living in a trailer. The ground actually belonged to my family at the time. My great-grandparents were black farmers who had land passed down to them from the previous generation. That was something special back in the '80s for people of color to actually own their own land, especially in a small country town like Princeton, Indiana. I loved four-wheeler riding, and I loved to go with my dad on the weekends and do the things he did. I went with him everywhere. I rode in the back of the tractor with him and Paw-Paw Toad, who was my dad's father, when they were farming. I remember picking watermelons in the summer heat, and sometimes shucking corn. I was honored to do it.

I was always trying to prove to my dad that I could do anything a boy could do. Somehow deep down I guess I sensed that he wanted to have a boy.

I had asthma really bad. My mother was always rushing me to the emergency room in the middle of the night. That sure didn't stop me from doing the things I loved to do, playing basketball and softball. I even played soccer one year, but I always had an asthma attack. That was just too much running. I really didn't care for soccer too much anyway. My mother always came to my games. She was very involved in everything I participated in.

We were raised in the church and grew up in Wayman Chapel on Lyles Station Road. From my remembrance we went every Sunday. I was always in Christmas and Easter programs and had speeches to memorize. Through it all, my mother had great faith. She took care of us the best she could. She loved us, spent time with us and, through the heartache and pain created by my dad, she still put a smile on her face and never took it out on us.

My dad had anger issues and the love and favoritism I once had for him grew very dim as I grew older and saw what was really going on. We went and stayed with my grandma quite a bit. The fighting just got worse. I was always afraid to go to sleep when my dad started one of his episodes. I felt so sorry for my mom and began to resent my dad. Hatred began to manifest inside of me.

I started acting out in school, getting kicked off of the bus at least once a week. Fighting with the boys and chasing the girls right alongside the boys. That's when my attraction for girls started to show. I wasn't quite sure why I felt the way I did; I just knew it was something I had to keep to myself.

Then I remember, after we left the trailer, we moved in my Uncle Butch's house on Lyles Station Road. This was property and land that was owned by my mother's side of the family. My Uncle Butch had passed away. We lived there for a few years. About this time in my childhood, Ashley was born. She was three years younger than me. Ashley and I could never get along. She was the complete opposite of me. She was super girly and didn't like to play sports, so we had absolutely nothing in common except for the fact that we got on each other's nerves. She always felt like I was the favorite child. I'm not sure why but evidently her reasons were valid. They were reasons she seemed to carry for many years. Erica was also born when she was around two years old. I was always ready to help my mom babysit. I loved being a big sister and I always wanted to help out my mom. Erica is a year older than Bre, so evidently my mother had to be pregnant at the time.

Boy, did she have her hands full. My dad was never around. She still managed to take me to all of my games and practices. I went out of town a lot for tournaments. I always went with my coaches, or Mr. Kolb, my grade school principal, would make sure I had an opportunity to go everywhere everyone else went. I loved Mr. Kolb. He was a very nice man. He seemed to take a special interest in me. I guess being really good at basketball helped and helping lead our team to Nationals almost every year made some impact on my teachers and coaches. That was a gift the Lord had blessed me with, and I walked in it all throughout my childhood.

I was sleeping on the couch on a Friday or Saturday night. I was waiting for the tooth fairy to put money under my pillow that night because I had just lost a tooth. My dad was the one who woke up extra early and put the money under my pillow. I was barely asleep when I heard him put money under my pillow. Then he quietly picked up the phone, called someone, and began to whisper. I heard him tell someone he would see them later. Then, right after he hung up, he called someone else and was speaking in his normal tone of voice.

My spirit was immediately alarmed. I had the feeling he was seeing another woman. I was so young. I'm not sure why I could discern that, but I did. When he made a phone call right after, talking in his normal tone, that let me know he was hiding something.

Shortly after that, he left. Mom got up and, as soon as she came into the living room, I told her what I had heard. I pretty much told her that dad was cheating. Mom then got us all dressed and loaded us all up in the car. She was pregnant at the time with Bre. We all went driving around with my mom. She was spying on my dad to see where he was going. I remember it like it was yesterday. We went driving down Lyles Station Road, and we saw my dad's truck parked at Bill Ashby's, a friend of my dad's.

I do recall my mom catching him once with another woman. They started yelling back and forth. I became extremely sad. I began to resent my dad even more. I felt sorry for my mom. It was then that I started to side with my mom and do everything I could possibly do to protect her. I could feel her and my dad becoming even more distant in their relationship. I felt like it was all my fault because I was the one who told Mom my dad was cheating. I'm sure she already had her speculations, she just didn't have any proof. That was most likely the icing on the cake.

Shortly after that, when I was in the fourth or fifth grade, our house caught on fire. I remember I had left one of those kerosene heaters on in my bedroom, something else I blamed on myself. So, me, Mom, and all my sisters moved back into Grandma's again. My dad moved in with Granny, so we were separated as a family. I remember everything was gone. We went to a neighbor's house and I remember looking out the window just watching our house burn down.

Grandma's was the place I knew as home. They had a full basement, one bedroom, one bathroom, and a kitchen. Mom slept in the living room. I loved that it was just us. Without my dad, there was no arguing, no fighting, and there was peace. I hated plugging my ears and singing to myself just to be able to fall asleep at night while my mom and my dad were arguing. At Grandma's it always smelled like laundry and water in the basement. I loved that smell. Even to this day those smells take me back to the days up on the hill.

By this time my sister Breann was born. Mom still worked at the power plant and made good money, so we were well taken care of. I always had the latest Jordan's and Reebok pumps. Life was good without my dad. I was still playing sports and Mom attended all of my games. I was always helping Mom with my little sisters. When we went back to school, Mom got these gift cards from work for us to go school shopping and we went out to eat and shopped till we dropped. We always went to Sizzler and ate. Eating out was a big thing for us. We didn't get to do that often. But I was blessed to have everything all the other kids had; name brands I never went without.

From this point on, my dad wasn't really in the picture. He was with his girlfriend and built a house where our trailer used to be. He started a new family. We would go visit my dad on the weekends and stay with him. He had another girl, Kalie, who was with his girlfriend. My parents finally divorced after 11 years of marriage. I didn't mind a bit. I hated seeing Mom go through the things she did. I loved my dad, but my mom showed us nothing but unconditional love through all of her pain and sacrifice. Mom had a quiet spirit, well-spoken, and highly educated. She always worked in a corporate environment and managed to get a business degree while raising us by herself. She never stopped going to church. As a result, she made it through hell and still managed to have the most loving Jesus smile I had ever seen.

My family on both sides struggled with alcohol. It was normal to see everyone drinking Budweiser on the holidays. That's how our family had a good time — no arguing or fighting or drama, just good old-fashioned partying. Most all in my family were high-functioning alcoholics. There were a few who could not function. Those were the things our family discretely swept under the rug. I came from a dysfunctional family because of the conflict and abuse my dad showed towards my mother.

I acted out in school and had failing grades from third grade all the way through. My mom would help me with my homework, but I would get impatient and give up altogether. She basically did it all for me. I just couldn't seem to retain things. I struggled immensely with schoolwork. I even had a hard time remembering the plays in basketball. I loved basketball. That was where my passion was. I remember being in the middle of a tournament and we would run our offensive plays and I would be so dumbfounded they had to take me out of the game. That was so embarrassing.

I was a tomboy, so I was tough. I wrestled and picked on some of the boys, not really sure why I felt as if I had to prove myself, but I did. When I went to visit my dad on the weekends, I would spend the summers on a four-wheeler, riding, going on adventures through the back roads out in the country. I loved four-wheeler riding. That was one of my favorite pasttimes. It was my escape from everything. My dad had bought me a three-wheeler. I literally rode that thing everywhere. I would go there on Fridays after school and ride until dark, then wake up at 5 a.m., pack a lunch, and roll out. My best friend at the time was Matt Greer. He was my riding buddy.

For my sixth grade dance, I went with Chris Cavins, my fake boyfriend at the time. I say fake because we just called ourselves that. We talked on the phone all night but never kissed. He was a white skinny guy with brown hair. He was in the eighth grade, so I thought I was doing big things, dating an older boy. I had always had a crush on Jeff Goldbach all through grade school, but I never had the nerve to tell him.

I remember I was on recess at Brumfield Elementary School, and purposely mentioned to one of the boys who played sports with Jeff that I liked him. One of his friends said," Black and white does not mix."

That statement crushed me all the way down to my soul. I felt very small and less-than. That's one of the reasons I went out with Chris. It made me feel as if I was worthy, and black and white could mix. I wasn't raised that way. I had some white in my family.

I had also always felt attracted to the most popular white girls in school, but never acted on it. I believe I was always much more attracted to the girls than the boys. I wasn't really sure why, but all I knew is that was the way I felt and I didn't feel like I could share those feelings with anyone. So, I didn't. It was just something else I kept inside, with all the other confusing and uneasy feelings and frustrations I was dealing with at that age.

We still lived at Grandma Alma's house in the basement. That was home for me and my sisters. Mom was still working at the power plant. She was also working out a plan for us to start a new life away from Princeton. That summer she told us we had to stay with my dad at Granny's house until school started back up. Grandma couldn't watch all four of us while school was out, so we were separated. We didn't want to stay with my dad for that long. We would miss my mom; anyway, my dad would always have Granny take care of us. We would be filthy from playing outside, and our hair wasn't done right. My dad didn't know how to do our hair and Mom hated how rough we would look after we stayed with him.

I remember something that has stayed with me my entire life, the promise Mom made to us when she dropped us off that summer. We asked Mom to promise she would come back to get us, and she did. She came by to see us every day after work. Granny's house was on the way to her job. She passed it every morning on her way to work and every evening on her way home. She hated having to deal with my dad just to visit us. He always tried to fight and argue with her. I wanted him just to leave her alone. By this time, he had realized Mom was moving on with her life without him and she was much happier.

My dad was having problems in his relationship. Grandpa Toad had died and my dad was all out of sorts, taking it out on Mom. Now, looking back, my dad was suffering from the consequences of the choices he made to step out of his marriage. Mom finally had peace. Mom showed up one day when summer was nearly over and came to rescue us. She kept the promise she had made to us and she said, "I will never leave you guys again."

And she never did.

She loved us so much! She showed us by doing what she said she would do and her commitment to visit us every chance she could, even though she had to go through hell to do it. What a sacrifice.

There is a memory that is unforgettable that I hold dear to my heart. In the sixth grade I went to a dance with my boyfriend at the time, Chris Cavins. I remember I wore a pair of brown stone-washed jeans and a pink and black button-up shirt I borrowed from my mom's closet. Nothing close to girly. Mom dropped me off at the dance and I had to leave by 8 p.m. because that was my bedtime. The dance ended at 9 p.m. Mom was pretty strict when it came to curfews and bedtime, so there was no negotiating. I remember a slow song came on, we were sitting on the bleachers, and Eric Clapton's "Tears in Heaven" started playing. Chris asked me to dance and I had never slow danced with a boy before. I said yes as my heart started beating 100 miles a minute. I remember being half-way through the song and here came Mom. As soon as I saw her, I pushed him away and took off walking towards her. She smiled and said, "You didn't have to push him away."

I guess I was embarrassed. I thought about it and I wasn't quite sure of my actions, but the next day I did apologize to Chris and told him I was nervous, which clearly had to have been the case. It was puppy love, the first boyfriend I ever had.

I remember when we left Granny's house, my mom said, "I have a big surprise for you guys."

We were all super excited.

She said, "How would you guys like to move to Evansville and go to another school and start all over again?"

We thought that sounded good, but then she said, "We are going on a family vacation to Disney World." We were so excited. That just made this new beginning sound really great.

Mom had left the power plant, gotten a us a beautiful townhouse in Evansville, and she had a boyfriend. Wow! A lot of surprises. But anything Mom had planned for us we knew we could count on. Mom had always kept her promises to us. We had never met this mystery man. Mom was introduced to him by Grandma and Aunt Carol at the horse races while we were with my dad. We had never been on a family vacation. This was like a dream come true.

I remember Mom taking us to Evansville to see our new home. It was late in the evening. I remember all of the lights in the city off of the highway. I remember like it was yesterday. I asked my mom if that was the ghetto. I was referring to all of the streetlights. I wasn't used to seeing so many lights. We lived out in the country, so it was fascinating to me. We had our trip to Disney World planned that summer right before school started in the fall. So, we settled into our new home. It was beautiful. Ashley and I shared a room, and Erica and Bre shared a room as well. It was a two-story townhome and the fact that we had our own beds and our own space was spectacular. We had brand new furniture, a living and family room. I felt as if we were living the life.

4

CHAPTER 4

A New Life

A new life: So I believed, so it was. Mom and Hugh made a new home for us to make new memories and have a normal life, a happy life.

We all transferred schools. I was attending Plaza Park Middle School on the east side of Evansville in a suburban neighborhood. I was in the middle of the semester and my transcripts had not yet been transferred, so my new school put me in an advanced literature class. In my old school, I was failing my math and science classes, and all of my other grades were low, although my teachers all had given me a C average all the way through. So, I was actually at an advantage and, because I had passing grades, I was able to play on the eighth grade team. Before that, I had gotten kicked off of the team until I got my grades up second semester of sixth grade year, so I was happy I got to do the only thing I loved to do — play basketball.

I remember telling the coaches my cousin was Travis Trice. He was a point guard at Ball State University. So that automatically gave me a starting position on the eighth grade team. Things were looking really great at this time.

There was a girl named Erica Maley. She was so kind to show me to all of my classes on my first few days of school. She took me under her wing and we actually became best friends. I seemed to have fit in with Erica, Alisha, and Chinyere. They were the girls I hung out with. We ate lunch together; that was my clique. Erica also played on the basketball team, so we seemed to have more in common than me and the other girls.

I was raised differently than the rest of the girls. My bedtime was still 8 o'clock, and we were not allowed to stay over at anyone's house unless my mother knew their parents. Erica and Alisha were into talking and dating guys, but I just wasn't there yet. My mind was on basketball and doing kid stuff. I spent that summer before freshman year hanging out with my family and school shopping. I was having a great time. My mother was my best friend. We would order pizza on Friday night and that was enough for me. We also went to Dairy Queen for dessert. We would always get our favorite blizzards. Life was good! We were all happy. No fighting and arguing. I was able to sleep sound every night. Finally, we were at peace, something I hadn't felt in a long time.

I remember one Sunday when my mom made dinner and invited everyone — Grandma and Aunt Carol. Mom was proud that she finally had a home she could call hers and quite frankly so was I. I remember exactly what was on the menu. She made her famous fried chicken, mashed potatoes, macaroni & cheese, and corn. For dessert, of course, she baked a cake. We had a feast, that's for sure. I hadn't seen or really even talked to any of my friends from school. I remember I called Erica a lot. She was always staying uptown with her friends who went to Bosse High School. I was not allowed to go uptown. It was in the hood and that's where all the "hoodlums" were.

THE END FROM THE BEGINNING

5

CHAPTER 5

Freshman Year

I remember the summer right before school started, I decided I wanted to start dressing like a girl. I figured high school would be a new beginning for a new me. I was tired of getting made fun of for dressing like a tomboy, and my big brother at the time suggested that if I wanted to fit in, that's what I should do. He was trying to help me. He introduced me to the older girls that he knew, so I started hanging out with them and they took me to Funky's. I had never been to a club before. If I'm not mistaken it was an 18-and-up club.

The girls he knew were seniors. Reagan and Meagan were actually related to me and were from Princeton.

They were all on the Varsity basketball team, and I was on the Freshman team. I was thinking, "I'm going to be popular and I have friends to hang out with." Well that wasn't the case. I wasn't in any of the same classes they were. I did have lunch with Erica and the girls she knew. We all sat at the table together — most all of the black kids. I knew a few of them, so I had friends for lunch. That was about the extent of it.

I went to school and was failing miserably. My math teacher, who was also my basketball coach, let me pass with a C. She told me I had to get my grades up or I was going to be benched second semester. I had every intention of doing just that. I worked really hard trying to get my math grade up and pull up my other grades as well, but the truth was starting to show. All the years of just passing by finally came to a head. Basketball was my life. It was something I was good at, and something I looked forward to. Nothing else really gave me as much joy as playing basketball. My identity was wrapped up in sports. I felt as if I was nothing without it. Riding four-wheelers was no longer an option, since we lived in the city now, and I didn't go and visit my dad anymore. I believe at this time he was in jail for back child support. We still went to Granny's on Christmas and opened presents with my dad's side of the family.

We now attended Nazarene Baptist Church. We became members in 1994. Mom took us to Sunday school, and church every Sunday morning. Mom had always kept her faith. We would get on our knees and pray the Lord's prayer every night, from when I was a baby until I was a sophomore in high school.

The Bible declares in Proverbs 22:6 (KJV): *"Train up a child in the way he should go: and when he is old he will not depart from it."*

Mom understood the importance of this particular scripture and, no matter what the circumstances were in her life, she wanted us to know Jesus. The only thing I had to stand on as far as faith was concerned, was the Jesus my grandmother knew, which was the same Jesus my mother knew. I was baptized when I was a child, but I didn't know Him for myself. The only relationship I had with the Lord was praying to a God I only heard about. By faith I knew He existed but wasn't sure how to follow Him. I knew a lot of things I had done as an adolescent He would not approve of, so I just did things out of self-will. Nothing really spiritual about it.

I had a friend, Samantha, who went to our church, and Mom knew her parents. I knew her mother was one of the mothers of the church that wore white on Sunday, and I believe her dad was one of the elders of the church. I spent the night with Samantha from time to time. She went to a different high school than I did though.

My sisters and I were very sheltered. We didn't have friends outside of school. I don't blame my mother at all for being strict, but it just made it harder for me to fit in with the other kids. The black girls didn't like me; they thought I acted "white" because I wasn't "city" like they were. Princeton was predominantly Caucasian, so those are the kind of kids I was used to being around. The black girls talked differently than I did. They said I talked "country." So right off the bat I was an outcast. The white girls really didn't accept me either, so I was in a territory all by myself.

6

CHAPTER 6

High School

Sophomore year was a lot different than freshman year. I started off on a bad foot. All of my grades were failing. All of the people I called my friends and ate lunch with had either dropped out or transferred to a new high school. I didn't make it through freshman forum, so I wasn't in any of the same classes as my peers. I knew absolutely no one. My lunch schedule was different than everyone I had sat with at lunch freshman year. I walked the halls and there was no one to talk to. I dreaded coming in every morning. Lunchtime was the absolute worst. I didn't want the humiliation of sitting by myself or of finally getting the nerve to actually ask someone if I could sit with them and they would say no. I was terrified of rejection, yet that had become a part of my daily life. As soon as I would hear the bell ring I would be starving and had to buy a candy bar because no food was allowed in the library. The only social life I had to look forward to actually being around my peers was lunch.

I was all alone. Depression was starting to kick in, and I thought to myself "Why am I even here? I don't have any friends; I'm failing all of my classes; my life is horrible."

After a couple weeks of going to the library, they didn't allow students to go to the library anymore. Wow! Everything was getting worse. I had to find somewhere to hide, so I took my candy bar to the bathroom and had lunch. I couldn't wait for the days to end. When they finally did, I had my mother and my younger sisters at least.

I remember my mom struggling to pay the bills. And my sister, Ashley, at this time had gone off the deep end. She was still dating Jeremy, Erica's baby brother. Ashley was 14 and would always find a way to sneak out of the house and stay with Jeremy's family. I remember my mom having to leave me with my younger sisters to go uptown — where we were never allowed to go — and hunt Ashley down. She would usually find her in the projects at Jeremy's older sister's apartment. Mom was getting to the point where she just couldn't handle Ashley and raise all of us.

Then the unthinkable happened — Ashley got pregnant by Jeremy. My mom had quit drinking, but at this time I remember her starting to drink again. Home life was now becoming stressful. I was trying to help Mom out with my younger sisters as much as I could, but I was going through it myself. I felt depressed, I felt rejected. I was not happy in life. I had nothing to look forward to anymore. I was starting to overeat and gain weight. I would always be running late in the mornings before school; my mom had to take Erica and Bre to school before I went, so I was always running behind. We were in a different school district now, so we didn't have a bus route, and my mom didn't want us to change schools.

My attendance was horrible because I started playing hooky and telling Mom to call in sick for me. I was getting in trouble for being late and I was suspended for my attendance. Mom went and explained to the principal the reason I was late every morning, so I was able to barely get by.

I came to a conclusion: I'm going to get a job and help my Mom with bills. My sisters needed things for basketball, so Mom allowed me to get a job. I loved working. I felt better about myself and it gave me something to look forward to, people to interact with me. I finally had a life. I worked as much as I possibly could.

I was helping Mom out, so she was thankful, and since I worked at a pizza place, we got to take home leftovers every night. My sisters looked forward to that. We had pizza a lot for dinner. My mom sent Ashley to live with my grandmother in Princeton so she could finish school and get the extra attention and discipline she needed. Mom was working a lot as well, trying to pay the bills. It was now just the four of us. Me and Ashley never really got along anyway. I loved her, but I didn't like her. The things she was doing stressing Mom out was a lot and very hard on all of us. My attendance at school was horrible. School became a last priority for me, and I rarely went to class anymore.

Mom was a secretary for a man named Robert who owned his own construction company. Really, she pretty much ran the company and he did the hands-on work. She also began to date him. He was a young, black, successful businessman. He was also divorced and very interested in mom. I remember her being able to work as much overtime as she wanted, so she did. The bills were paid, we had everything we needed for the first time in a long time. We seemed to be financially stable and Mom was happy.

Robert had a niece named Valerie, and we became really good friends. She was two years older than me. She drove a red Mustang. I thought she was really cool. Finally, I had a friend, someone who accepted me for who I was and actually wanted to hang around me. We became the best of friends. In fact, she was my only friend, so I held on pretty tight. I remember we would talk on the phone for hours. We started hanging out every weekend. Now I had a life. She was always trying to talk to guys and I was just along for the ride. We would cruise around and listen to music. I was finally a part of something. I had a social life. I was very impressionable. I was a follower, not a leader. Someone could lead me in a dark dungeon and, as desperate as I was to fit in, I would probably go. Looking back, it was sad really. I wasn't depressed anymore. This was the only happiness I knew. So, we hung pretty tight for about six months. She was supposed to start at University of Southern Indiana in the fall. She started her first semester classes and I was skipping my sophomore classes to hang out with her.

Then suddenly my whole world was turned upside down! Valerie started hanging around her older cousin and pretty much ditched me. I would call her every day and her mom would tell me she was asleep or she was out. It took a while for me to figure out she was ignoring my calls and no longer wanted to hang out with me. At this time, my principal wanted to expel me from Harrison and send me to a secondary school, Stanley Hall. So, I was expelled from school, my best friend ditched me, and I was slipping into a deep depression. I had nothing to look forward to and literally my life sucked. My mom made me go to this secondary school and expected me to graduate.

She drove Robert's car, a Volvo with tinted windows. I didn't have a license, but I was in Driver's Ed class and had my permit at the age of 15, so my mother allowed me to drive the Volvo to and from school and pretty much anywhere else I had to go. I thought I was hot stuff. I was driving a luxury car with a cellphone in it. Back in the 90s only wealthy people had cellphones. Pagers were the style. Actually, we referred to them as beepers and everyone wore them, including myself.

So, I started this new school and I felt good about myself. I drove to school every day and it made me feel some type of way about myself. Around this time, I was let go from Denny's for being late too many times. I believe I began to work weekends only at Sabarro's and wasn't applying myself in school or being dedicated to my job as I was in the past. I had a "just-passing-through" attitude about life — no goals or aspirations for myself. Nothing to look forward to or be a part of. I was bound to fall sometime soon. I had no direction. Any direction would be better than the way I was going. I was on a road of unhappiness and loneliness.

Then my mom and Robert broke up. Mom had no job, no vehicle, and our place of stability was slowly but surely decreasing. Mom began to drink. I have this unforgettable memory of me sitting on the steps, depressed, looking to the sky for answers to the questions I didn't know how to ask, or for that matter, who to ask.

My mother evidently didn't know the answers either.

She was in a wilderness I knew nothing about. Apparently, I was too. She asked me if I wanted a beer and I took a sip for the first time. That's the only thing she knew to reach for in this season to cope, to deal with the pain she was experiencing at the time. The pain had to have been great for her to turn back to alcohol. I thought it was nasty, but I drank it anyway. I'm sure I had some kind of buzz going on.

Something spectacular took place in the next few months. I remember my mom going to Expressway Dodge to get a car. Evidently her credit had been built up. She was approved, not only a car for her, but for me too. She test-drove a brand new 1998 Plymouth Breeze and I test drove a brand new 1998 Dodge Neon. We left that day with both cars.

I remember sitting on my front porch just admiring my brand-new car. I saw a little dirt on the driver's side door, so I took a paper towel and wiped it clean. I remember telling myself, "I'm going to have to get a job if I'm going to keep this car." It gave me purpose. Now I had a reason to go to work and something to be responsible for.

I had just started going to this secondary school, Stanley Hall, and I immediately met people who were receptive and wanted to talk and socialize. I immediately felt like I would fit in at this school. I remember leaving school around 11:30 a.m. every day, blasting my radio listening to "Master P" and "Montell Jordan." I was really into rap and R&B in this era of my life.

I started a part-time job as a cashier at Ben Franklin Crafts. I would get out of school and go directly to work in the afternoon. I immediately made friends with Laura. She was a student at University of Evansville who wanted to be a teacher. Her parents were well-to-do. She was from St. Louis and they paid for her to live in a very nice one-bedroom apartment off of campus. She was 21, tall, thin, and she smoked Kool's. I thought she was one of the coolest chicks I had ever met. She had this walk full of stride that was boasting with confidence, and this smile that was so genuine and inviting. I could be myself around her. We just clicked. I remember on Sundays she would be like, "Let's go get some good food somewhere, on me." She had two American Express cards she could use at her leisure. She would give me one to pay for my meal. I had never had access to anything like that. I personally thought she had it made.

I remember I asked her to give me a hit off of her cigarette a couple of times and choked. She just laughed at me. Before you knew it, I was buying my own pack of cigarettes. I justified my smoking by trying to lose weight, and I was dieting, so it seemed to be working. I started feeling good about myself. I had a car, a job, and a cool friend. Since she was 21, she and her friends always went to O' Brians, which was a pool hall. She loved to go play pool, drink beer, and listen to music. I thought I was hot stuff, hanging in a bar, drinking beer. My social life went from non-existent to having cool friends and barhopping. I was so desperate to fit in.

I have this unforgettable memory that I can still see. It was a memory I would visit from time to time: being fully content and full of joy. I was satisfied in this moment. I felt good about myself and life was actually good.

I was 18 years old. I had just gotten off work, got in my brand-new car headed down the Lloyd Expressway on my way home, listening to "Let's Ride," Master P and Montell Jordan. My bass was all the way up, I was beating on the steering wheel to the beat of the music, loving my life.

I was truly happy in that moment. That was a moment I had to pull from many times over the years. I don't remember having many memories where I felt happiness. That's sad really, but it is what it is.

So, I began drinking socially just to fit in. This is where it all began. Laura was my only friend. We hung out and worked together. I believe she was my first girl crush, but I wouldn't even think about acting on it. Now, thinking back, I was attracted to her in more than one way. She had a boyfriend named Chuck who she talked about all the time, so there was no way I would even think about it.

I remember second semester at Stanley Hall, Chasity South was the prettiest and most popular girl there and

I was drawn to her. She asked me for a ride a couple of times and before you know it, we were inseparable and became best friends. Chasity would always invite me to go out to lunch with her at her favorite place, Los Bravos.

Of course, we clicked.

7

CHAPTER 7

Highway to Hell

I needed a friend and Chasity needed a friend with a car. It was convenient for both of us. She had a life and friends and I had a ride to take us wherever we desired to go. She would stay at her Uncle's and his girlfriend's. They were a younger couple and didn't mind if we all came over to party. They would blast the music and they were so much fun. I had never been to a real party. I felt like I was finally living life to the fullest. I remember they would be drinking gin and orange juice. I hated the taste of gin. I think I poured out most of mine and just pretended to drink it to fit in. It would be Ricky, Alisha, Chasity, Erica, Trisha and me.

One evening I was acting like I was too intoxicated to drive so I could stay the night with her. She had a money man named Jon who always went to the club to watch her dance and gave her free crank. She had a bag of it for us to do in the morning before school. So, I crashed on the couch and in the morning when we woke up, we did a line. I can honestly say, from the euphoria I felt off of that line of crank, I instantly fell in love with it. I remember feeling like I was going a million miles an hour as I was driving my blue Neon trying to get us both to school on time. I remember making a left turn at a red light, then halfway through the light I saw the sign, plain as day, "No Left Turn."

I ran that light and all I remember is us both busting up laughing. We were higher than a kite. I felt so good in that moment. She told me it made her focus on her homework more and we got a lot of homework done that day because we were on speed, "geekin" on our homework.

That was the beginning of addiction for me, a battle that I would go on to fight for many years to come. The door was opened and just welcomed me in like it had been waiting for me to just come on in. As I made my way in, the steel bars of an unseen prison shut quickly and there was no key. I was going to be in bondage for 16 years and didn't even know it. Drinking and doing crank occasionally became a part of my story. I was on a highway to hell and I was going really fast down it.

Now I no longer had a job. I needed one. Mom gave me money to spend, but I still had a $200 car payment that she could not afford, and the lifestyle I was living now consisted of blowing money. I recall Chasity mentioned I should dance with her and make easy money. I took it as kind of a dare, so one day I went home and took some lingerie out of my mom's drawer. The closest thing I could find to sexy. Me, sexy? Yeah, right! I was this tomboy who walked country and couldn't dance to save my life.

So, I drove to the She Lounge in my blue Neon with my mother's lingerie and headed to the strip club at 11:30 in the morning and tried out.

I remember before I went up, they told me I had to come up with a stage name. One of the waitresses walked by and said, "Destiny."

Destiny it was.

Looking back, what in the heck was I doing?

Who was I? I wasn't raised this way. Had I completely lost my mind? Apparently.

I picked out a song to audition. The D.J. at the time was Terry. She was a butch-looking chick, heavy set, mullet haircut. She was cool though.

I loved Aerosmith so I picked one of their songs. This particular club had a lot of motorcycle guys and construction workers and rock & roll was the type of music they liked. It was a predominantly Caucasian club. Story of my life. I'm not sure why, but I felt as if I was more accepted by Caucasians than my own race, or maybe the rejection I experienced in high school from the black girls caused me to not really interact with them. This left no room for them to even try to get to know me.

I didn't own any high heels. All I wore was tennis shoes.

They said over the microphone, "Destiny to the stage." I got on that stage in lingerie and socks. I was nervous and offbeat.

The second song you were supposed to drop your top, so I did. I was completely sober and did what I had to do. When the song was over, I got off stage and they told me to start that night. I was excited. I immediately drove straight to Chasity's to tell her the good news. She couldn't believe it.

She was like, "Great! We can ride to work together tonight."

In reality I just opened up another door, stepping into the darkness that invited me in. I had just stepped into another prison cell that led to sexual perversion.

Again, I would be in bondage for the next 16 years. I was being completely led by Darkness and didn't even realize it. It was so easy to just keep falling into sin. I had morals and values that just completely disappeared.

Destiny and Monet. Those were our stage names. We were a dangerous pair. We were the best of friends, completely inseparable. If you saw her then you saw me.

I hardly ever stayed at home anymore. My mother must have been devastated. I just completely bailed on all of my responsibilities and left her out to dry. I was so selfish now. Her two daughters were now living a rebellious life and nowhere near the right path. She didn't deserve that at all. The sacrifices she had made for us and the love she showed us throughout the years was not the love we were giving her in return.

I remember her chasing me down on a Saturday. She showed up and, without embarrassing me, told me to get my behind home immediately. She had to work and needed me to watch my sisters.

Chasity told me, "You shouldn't have to be responsible for your sisters. They're not your kids. They are not your responsibility."

In reality, maybe not, but I owed it to my mother to help her out and it was my responsibility. I lived in her house. She was still taking care of me. I decided to take Chasity's advice and believe that.

Our upbringing was totally different to her. That may have been, but my Mom always said, "We are a TEAM!"

We always had been.

At that time of my life I was not being a team player for sure. I was being very selfish and led astray.

Soon after that, Chasity and I got our own place on Florida Street, a block away from her mother. So, we were stripping, drinking, and drugging.

My life was quickly spiraling out of control at this point. Mom had two sets of furniture. She had been keeping our old family room furniture in Robert's garage. When she and Robert split, he dropped the furniture off and it was now pretty much on top of our living room furniture.

Mom was very depressed at this time, I could tell. She began drinking again. She was jobless since she didn't work for Robert anymore and, on top of that, Ashley was sent to my grandmother's, and I was running the streets now acting like a hoodlum. This was a tough time for my mother. I should have been there for her. Instead, I got this bright idea one day that since I was moving in with Chasity and we had no furniture, so I decided I would just empty out Mom's extra furniture while she was at work and take it off of her hands.

Big mistake!

Mom was heated when she found out what I had done. She told me to bring back her furniture, that same day. It was the way I went about things that made her mad. Looking back, that was so shady. I knew better than that. I should have asked permission. I knew she would say no. That's why I took it.

This part of my life is kind of blurry. I was drinking every day and was miserable. I didn't feel good about myself at all. The alcohol had already had a hold on me, and the drugs were becoming more of a problem.

I was in full-blown addiction.

CHAPTER 8

Facing Addiction Head On

I lost my job, then, shortly after, my car was repossessed. I went as far as hiding my car way out in the country so they could not find it. They would show up at my house and I would act like I wasn't myself and I had no idea what was going on. I kept that going for a while and one of the people that called my phone asking me to give them the car told me that, if I didn't give them my car, they would take my mother's car. That was a deal breaker for me, so I had one of the repo guys follow me out in the country and I gave them the keys.

I remember falling into a deep depression. What was I going to do now? No one wants to be around someone who has no money, no job, and a bad attitude. Chasity just found out she was pregnant and she was going to be a mother now, not a stripper. By then I was already dependent on alcohol and drugs and just up and quitting was something I couldn't do at this time. So, she quit working and I didn't want to go dance all by myself. Our lifestyles were completely opposite.

Rent was due and I couldn't take on that responsibility. I had just had a car repossession. I was completely irresponsible and unwilling to change. I did everything Chasity told me to do, but this change was something I had no control over.

Truth be told, I was secretly in love with her and she was taken. The closeness we shared with each other was extremely unhealthy and that was why. We never slept together but the feeling I had for her was a physical and emotional attraction I could not share with her. I just kept the thoughts to myself.

Everything was falling apart, and I was a complete mess. We started arguing daily because I was always drunk and, now that she was sober, we were not a good mix. She decided she was going to go to a shelter where pregnant women could go and get the help and support they needed to get on their feet and be able to support their children. It was a perfect idea and definitely going to be good for the both of them, but that left me all alone.

I had pretty much neglected my family and now I was in a worse position than I was before. I was no longer a sweet, innocent young lady who put her family first and a team player in helping her mother. I was now a jobless, miserable, depressed addict, and belligerent alcoholic. The devil had succeeded in putting me on this destructive path. I had no idea on how to turn back. I was literally in a prison and I didn't have the key. I had suppressed all of my hurt, failure, and pain. I was walking around lost in the sauce. I even went so far as believing every lie the enemy sold me on; maybe someday Chasity and I would be together and we would live happily ever after. But that was crazy. I was in a relationship all by myself and was heartbroken. I would ask myself: "Why do I have these feelings? Am I gay? What is wrong with me?"

I was in a battle and didn't know it. I was fighting a spiritual battle internally. I was raised in the church. The Word of God was planted in me as a child. I knew right from wrong, so the conviction felt as real as the lies I heard from the enemy. The lies were always easier and louder than that small still voice, the Holy Spirit inside of me. Even as a child, my flesh overruled my emotions, and this desire for women would eventually show itself. I had fought it my whole life and it became a reality when I found myself secretly in love with my best friend. Finally, for that time in my life, I was put out of my misery. Chasity was moving on and that put me out of the picture. I was stuck in a dark hole. I tried to hold on to her and that toxic friendship for dear life.

I was going to have to fight this battle alone. I couldn't go back to my mother's. She had lost her house and was living in Princeton at Grandma's.

Our friend, Trisha, who Chasity had gone to high school with, had been partying with us on the side-lines ever since we stayed at Ricky and Alisha's. Trisha dibbled and dabbled in drugs just like we did. She had a boyfriend who was a cocaine dealer and they lived together. She had broken up with this guy and was pregnant with his baby. Her boyfriend went to jail on drug charges. So, she applied for low-income housing, and, since she was pregnant, she was able to move in Carriage House Apartments. Trisha knew nothing about taking care of a baby. She was like a big kid herself. So, when she had her baby, she told me I could move in rent free and get a job. Chasity had a new job at Vanguard Answering Service and she got me on with her. So, I worked nights and Chasity worked days. She had me watch Graydon, her brand-new son, while she worked during the day.

Evidently, Chasity owed her mom quite a bit of money for helping us out with back rent. Her mother was adamant about her paying her back. So, Chasity decided she was going to work and pay her mother her debts and use my money to furnish her new apartment. She was there when I cashed my check. Actually, she cashed it at her bank for me, gave me what I needed to get by, and put the rest toward her layaway furniture for her apartment when it became available. I was dumb enough to let her take all my money. Chasity always had a way of manipulating me in every way possible for her benefit. Being the Kristin who let people run all over me, I did just that. People always took my kindness for weakness, but I let them.

Trisha didn't want to be alone and neither did I. We were both a lot alike. She had a passive personality and was very easy to get along with. She wasn't intimidating and wasn't controlling. We became very close really fast. She was easy to love and never tried to take advantage of me. She was actually a blessing to me.

Since I worked second shift she let me sleep in her bed. She couldn't wait for me to get home every night, so I could get Morgan to sleep for her. I would go upstairs and get her out of her crib, sit with her in a rocking chair, and rock her to sleep every night. I felt good about myself being needed and helping her take care of her baby. When Morgan would fall asleep, I would change her and put her in her crib and go downstairs, drink a few beers, and go to sleep. That was my daily routine. Trisha needed me just as much as I needed her, so it worked out.

I felt as if I needed to run as far away as I could, but where would I go? I decided to call my cousin, Justin. He had visited me recently at me and Chasity's. We ended up getting really drunk and he went back home. So, I called him and just poured my heart out to him, asking him for advice on how to fix my life. His answer was, "Why don't you come to Manhattan, Kansas with me?" That sounded to me like a great escape. I had never been to Kansas, so I was like, "Come and get me." I had nowhere to go. I just wanted to run away. With everything I had been through in my life, this was the worst it had ever been. I was living a reckless and destructive life. All the morals and values I once had disappeared. I had no idea who I was.

9

CHAPTER 9

Kansas, Here I Come

I remember I wanted to leave Chasity something that she could always remember me by. I had a friendship necklace engraved at Droste's Jewelers, one of the most expensive jewelry stores in the state of Indiana. It had a broken heart; one piece had her name engraved and the other piece had mine. That necklace ended up costing me more than $200, and that was all the money I had to my name. That was just my heart. I always gave it to the wrong people.

The Lord had given me that revelation 20 years later: *"Give not that which is holy unto the dogs, neither cast ye your pearls before swine, lest they trample them under their feet, and turn again and rend you"* (Matthew 7:6 KJV).

Justin came to pick me up on a Friday night. We got sloppy drunk. Chasity was supposed to come and spend the night with me. Instead she stood me up and didn't show until the next morning. I reeked of alcohol and said my goodbyes. That was a very sad day for me. I was going in the condition I was in, thinking I would have a fresh start in a different state and would soon find happiness.

Boy was I wrong!

I remember my mother always telling me, "No matter where you go, you always take yourself with you, and it is yourself you have to deal with."

She was right. Even though I was moving to a different state, I still had my addictions and destructive behavior right behind me.

You can run but you can't hide.

So, we drove to Manhattan, Kansas and I went to live with him and his wife Gina. They were both in the army and were stationed at Fort Riley but had decided to live off base because they were married.

I stayed in the house for about a week, slept most of the days and tried to get my mind right. I would go take a dip in the swimming pool every now and then, and when Justin and Gina came home in the evenings, me and Justin would drink beer all night. They would leave me some cigarettes to smoke for the day and I would have all day to think.

I got the bright idea I would get a job at Bobby T's. It was like a sports bar and wings joint. They partied on the weekends. A college was right down the street. So, I worked there for a couple of weeks and I got caught drinking on a Friday night and was on probation for 30 days. If I was to get caught drinking again, I would be terminated.

I was 20 years old, not yet the legal age to drink.

A bunch of people I knew went to an event that I wasn't scheduled to work, so I was just hanging out.

It was like 11 p.m. and I was wanting a beer. Everyone around me was having a great time. Someone offered to buy me a drink, so I snuck it. I was kicked out and couldn't continue to work there anymore. So now I had to get a job somewhere else. My drinking was really starting to get the best of me and I was now accustomed to this party lifestyle. I decided I was going to get a job as a stripper because there was a strip club near the base and they thought I could make a lot of money off of the guys in the Army.

I was continuing to practice my destructive patterns. This idea of recreating myself was now turning me into an even bigger monster than I already had become.

I had Justin's wife Gina go with me to the strip club. I got a job and started immediately. Gina did my makeup and made sure that everything was okay. She came with me like three nights in a row, sat at a table, and stayed until my shift was over. I was now comfortable enough to drive to and from work by myself, so I did. Justin and Gina had a hunter green two-door Ranger pickup truck they allowed me to drive since I worked second shift. I was able to have transportation, since they worked first shift. That lasted for a while, and I made some really good money, but I was so unhappy. I began to drink even more. There were no drugs I could get hold of, so I wasn't using. If I had known a dealer I would have definitely made it happen.

Justin and Gina were having problems in their marriage, so I was stuck in the middle of an everyday drama that just made life even harder for me to deal with. Gina moved out, so it was just me and Justin, and he was a mess.

I decided I couldn't make a life for myself. This was not the fresh start I thought it would. I had been gone about five months and I was extremely homesick. I had been hanging out with Justin on base with him and his buddies. So, I got a bus ticket and went back home to Indiana.

My mother now lived in a three-bedroom house in Princeton with my sisters on Spring Street. It was a very nice home. Mom was excited to have me back. I made it back to Evansville and Chasity was the first visit I made. I wanted to see her and Graydon. Noah, the father of Graydon, was now living with her and they were raising him as a family, which was good. I was so happy to see her. I had been like an aunt to Graydon ever since he was born. I used to buy him onesies and take care of him while she was working. I loved that little guy.

While I was living with Mom in Princeton, I remember somehow, some way I got hold of some meth. I smoked dope in my room almost every day. I would clean the house from top to bottom, wash the walls, and shampoo the carpet. I was hanging out with my sister, Ashley. She was attending Princeton High School. She was raising Ellie and living with her boyfriend, Steve. Jeremy was in a detention center for minors. He had gotten into some legal trouble and he and Ashley separated. A friend of Ashley's dated a dope cook, so she had an unlimited supply of anhydrous dope which was really strong and highly addictive. That's what I was getting strung out on.

I didn't have a job yet, so I had more than enough time to get high while my mom was at work. Ashley already had all the drug connections I needed to stay high. Ashley and I never got along before, but now that we were doing drugs together we seemed to be forming some kind of relationship — very unhealthy, obviously, since drugs were involved.

Mom worked in Evansville at C.A.P.E (Community Action Program of Evansville) as the Grandparents Director. There was an energy-assistance program throughout the winter months, so it was seasonal —

November to March. It was a data-entry job, helping low-income families with government funds. Since Mom had a very good work ethic and was a person of influence there, I was immediately hired and took my addiction with me. At this time Mom had no idea I was using drugs. She knew I drank every night, but she was also drinking at this time in her life.

Mom still had that 1998 Red Plymouth Breeze and she thought that we could ride back and forth to work together. Mom never missed work, so I pretty much had it made. I remember Mom waking me up every morning just like she did when I was in high school. I would drink anywhere from six to eight beers every single night. Mom would try and tell me to slow down so I wouldn't get drunk and have a hangover every morning.

I remember Kristy, a friend that I knew through Chasity, came in with pair of brand-new Air Max's and a beautiful gold chain. She was a drug dealer, so we worked out a deal where I could go over to her house on my lunch and get high. She wasn't too far from my work. She came to drop me off a sack of some really good stuff for free, knowing when I ran out I would come to her and buy some more.

So on Fridays, as soon as I cashed my paycheck, I put my order in for a couple grams, and she came to deliver — Johnny on the spot. I now had access to meth. I was smoking every day. I would get high before work, on my lunch, and sometimes after work. I would try not to get high in the evenings. I needed to come down so I could make it to work every day. I would get drunk and pass out and have a pick-me-up in the morning. My addiction was full-blown. I don't see how I kept it from everyone for so long. My mom had no idea I was on anything other than alcohol.

I had this friend named Cindy. She was in her late thirties and I was just in my early twenties. She knew I was getting high and that was right up her alley. She was no stranger to meth. She and her husband lived on the west side of Evansville in a very suburban, predominantly Caucasian neighborhood. Cindy was my road dog. We got along very well. She was fun and outgoing just like I was. We both liked to party. She always went home and let her dogs out on her lunch, so I would load up the pipe and we would smoke. We would come back to work and do our job. We made that an everyday routine.

Around March, when energy assistance ended, there was an opening for the VISTA program, which was a national service program designed to alleviate poverty. President Kennedy originated the idea for Volunteers in Service to America incorporated into the Ameri-Corps network of programs.

I easily got that job because CAPE was affiliated with them. Our office was off of Virginia Street in a Catholic church. We would be in the Learning Center at CAPE. I really didn't want to be in the CAPE office, because I was high and the ladies I was working with seemed to have it out for me from the beginning. My mom had a position in the office and they were jealous of that as well, when there was no reason for that. So, I felt really uncomfortable in the CAPE office, and the monotony was unbearable. I went to the other office a few miles away and just did my work in that building.

Looking back, I was also isolating myself. When you are on drugs, you don't want to be around people that are not on drugs. There was another lady named Ruth who also was a VISTA volunteer and she was open to doing a little line every once in a while, so we began to hang out and became good friends. We would go to her house and get high on lunch. So, I provided the dope and I found a friend who provided a place to do it, which was vital because I lived all the way in Princeton.

We had a trip coming up in Chicago, Illinois for training. Everything was paid for. I would not leave Evansville, Indiana without seeing my dope man first. I was so dependent on that drug I could not leave for a few days without a bag. It was sad, really. I made it to Chicago after catching a later flight because I had to wait on my dope man to show up.

I arrived around 11 p.m. I had a roommate who was in bed sleeping when I arrived. I had gotten high at the airport. I came in the room and started ironing my clothes. My roommate woke up. I wasn't discrete at all. I was smoking a foil and I asked her if she wanted some.

She said no, so I was like, "More for me!"

I skipped almost every training breakfast because I had partied all night the night before and had a tremendous hangover. My co-workers saw me hanging out with this girl from Chicago. We were at the Karaoke bar, so drunk we had to hold each other up. Of course, they used that as ammunition against me, and I overheard them gossiping about me when I went to their room looking for Ruth. I overheard them saying that I was gay and probably spent the night with that white girl I partied with.

After the retreat, they really started acting shady towards me and it began to really affect me in a negative way. I didn't even want to go to work anymore, so I came in, showed my face, and went to Kristy's house to smoke my problems away.

At that time, I was still living in Princeton with my mom. Ashley and Ellie were living there too. Ashley was dating a guy named Steve. He owned a car detailing shop and was much older than Ashley. He was around 30 and Ashley was 18. He liked Ashley so much. He took care of her and let her drive his car. He hired my dad to work with him in the shop because my dad had just gotten out of prison for back child support and needed a job. Him and Steve became good friends. Steve had a best friend named Perry. He lived in Henderson, but him and Steve hung out pretty tight. He tried to get Steve to hook him up with me. At this time, I had a super huge crush on Chance, Chasity's older brother.

I had known him for years, as long as me and Chasity had been friends. I also thought he was good-looking. He had just split up with Sabrina, the mother of all of his children. I knew their family well enough to know him and Sabrina had been together all through high school. They were like as young as 15 when they first started dating.

So, me and Chance were getting high together and were both getting our drugs from the same connection, which made it to where we spent a lot of time together. I remember we were just hanging out and he came and picked me up from Princeton and took me over to his mother's house, which she was okay with to a certain extent. Chance and I were both confused and hurting, so that was the connection we had. I started hanging out with him almost every day. We never slept together, but it was getting to that point I kind of wanted to, but was too shy to initiate the whole thing and Chance was a gentleman and very sweet. But I also knew the other side of him, which could be violent when he drank, so I was kind of torn between the two.

We were having a good time partying, using, and suppressing everything that was hurting us and all the things we were unable to deal with. He was in just as bad a shape as I was, so I thought maybe we were a perfect match.

One day I went over to his mother's house on my lunch and knocked on the basement window because

I knew he would be down there. He wasn't working at the time and I wanted to hang out and get high, so I brought some dope over. He had company that day. Kelly was one of Kristy's friends and evidently she and Chance had just hooked up because they were lying on the couch together and Chance certainly wasn't trying to hide anything. We had never been together sexually, so I really couldn't react, but it did hurt my feelings. I would never be bold enough to admit or even act like it bothered me. I had learned never to show my emotions. If I was upset or hurt, I sure wasn't going to show it. That was a wall that I had put up many years ago, a learned behavior. I would never cry in front of anyone. I would always cry in secret. So that was the end of me and Chance or whatever was going on between us.

I started talking to Perry, Steve's friend. He was extremely attractive, tall, slender build, beautiful blue eyes, short brown hair, very well dressed. I was like, "Sure, why not?" He took me out on a couple of dates. We went out with my friends at Gloria's Corral Club and drank and had a good time. He had mostly black friends, so he was used to a different crowd. I had all white friends, so our circles were completely different. I don't think he even really liked the places I took him out to, so we didn't really mesh well together to begin with. I did like to show him off though, especially around Chance. I really liked making him jealous. I still liked Chance, even though I was dating Perry.

So anyway, a little time passed and my sister and her boyfriend were evidently having difficulties, because I found out her and Perry were seeing each other behind the scenes. So that was it for me. I was upset for a little while. Mom knew about it, because I caught him and Ashley talking on the phone. I had Mom pick up the phone because I had that feeling. Mom picked up the landline and went and addressed Ashley. It was a big deal. In the midst of that drama, Steve came over, beating on the door, with all of Ashley's things and told us what he had found out. Evidently him and Perry already had a blowout about it and the crap had hit the fan. So, Ashley and Ellie got kicked out and went to live with Perry in Henderson. I just got really drunk, cried all night and that was the end of it.

I was getting heavier and heavier in my addiction. I ended up getting really sick with mono and was in bed for 30 days. I got it from smoking dope with so many people using the same paraphernalia, plus I had been up for so many days, my immune system was weak and could not fight off the sickness. Luckily, I lived with Mom and worked with Mom, so she let everyone know I was very ill and could not get out of bed. I lost a lot of weight because all I did was sleep and I didn't have an appetite. The doctor had me on Tylenol with codeine. I was prescribed that for over a month and I remember loving that stuff and made sure I didn't run out. I had a very addictive personality. I was so sick, I had no desire to do any meth or drink any alcohol, but I stayed full of that codeine. I remember waking up one day and telling myself, "I'm ready to do some meth and get back up on my feet." I had enough strength and I was feeling much better.

I'm not quite sure of the situation, but I do remember my mom finding a bag of meth. It must have fallen out of my backpack because she found it and immediately told me she was going to flush it down the toilet. I lied to her real quick. Frantically I told her it was Chance's and I was holding it for him and if she flushed it, I would have to pay $50 that I did not have. So, she gave it back to me. I'm not sure if she believed me or not, but that was my personal sack and I couldn't part with it. I hadn't gotten high in a long time and I was more than ready.

I eventually went back to work and continued hanging out with the same people, living the same life. A few months later the Energy Assistance program ended until the next year, so we moved into Stone-hedge apartments on the east side. These were really nice townhouses. I decided to get a job at Golden Corral. I was 23 at the time. I really liked working at Golden Corral and I made really good money. It was a buffet, so it was a lot easier than waiting tables. I made friends with Shelly. She was 10 or 15 years older than me. When Ashley, my sister, worked there they would hang out and get high. You know what they say, birds from the same feather flock together. Shelly and I had something in common; we both liked meth. So now I had another permanent drug connection. Everywhere I went I would always end up finding friends and connections. I guess that's what addicts do in an addict world. Me and Shelly hung really tight. She had a really nice house with her boyfriend, so I would go over to her house and we would get high all night, play cards, and go in to work together the next day.

A few months went by and I started being good friends with this Hispanic girl named Olga. She was gay and originally from Texas. We became really close.

I noticed this beautiful girl named Aimee. When I saw her for the first time, I knew I wanted to be with her. She was 17 and she already had a girlfriend. Aimee had the most beautiful smile, and this laugh I fell in love with. I told Olga about the crush I had on Aimee because I wanted Olga to tell her for me. I had never been as attracted to a woman as much as I was attracted to her. I wanted to wait until she turned 18 first, because I was 23. We became work buddies and we were getting to know each other as friends. She went to beauty school during the week, so I only got to see her on the weekends. I waited for her to come in every Friday and Saturday night. She would come through the doors with this bright yellow jacket and, as soon as I laid eyes on her, my heart would drop to my stomach. I was completely head over heels in love with this girl. It made my day just to see her. I knew that she was a good girl and wouldn't like me if I was on drugs, so I waited until after the weekend when she didn't come to work to get high. I didn't want to be high around her because I didn't have much of a personality on meth and I wanted her to see the real me. I knew I was going to be with her. It was just a matter of time. She ended up breaking up with her girlfriend, but she came in to see Aimee one day and I was like, "OMG!"

I expected her girlfriend to be just as young and beautiful as Aimee, and I wasn't confident enough to make a move. I needed to see what I was competing with. When I saw Crystal, I was like, "I'm making my move," because I didn't feel as if I had to compete anymore. I told Olga to invite her out to the gay club with us. I had planned to make my move. We danced and had a good time. I wasn't going to stop until she was completely mine. I was in love for the first time in my life, and we hadn't even kissed yet.

I remember we went out one night and she came over. My mom didn't mind. She had no idea I was into girls, so we were able to spend time together at my house. Mom was always in her room watching TV so we would hang out. When she left that night, I walked her out of the door and we kissed for the first time. It was like in a movie — that scene where, when someone kisses someone and shuts the door, they just pause and stay in that moment. I was so taken. That was the first time I ever kissed a girl, and I liked it.

I replayed that kiss in my mind for several days.

Soon after that, Aimee and I were spending a lot of time together. I think my whole heart was in it. She was just young, having a good time. I felt as if I could spend the rest of my life with her. I had fallen for her for real and there was nothing I could do about it. I think she had been with her ex-girlfriend for like five years and she wasn't really trying to be tied down at such a young age. That wasn't the case for me, so we continued to carry on this relationship that wasn't completely sealed yet; but in my mind, I was working on that.

I started to go to the gay club with Olga like two or three times a week. We were always chasing after women, going to the strip and gay clubs, just living it up.

Olga was a little older than I. I was 23; she was 29.

She had a really nice car so we had transportation and she liked to chase women like I did. We became the best of friends. I finally could be open about my feelings with someone who felt the same feelings as I did. Olga had "come out" so to speak. I wasn't ready for all that yet but at this time in my life I knew I would never go back to men.

Olga used to teach me Spanish. There was this word we would use all the time, "momacita," which meant "hot momma." To address an attractive, or gorgeous woman in Latin America, that was the word to use. We would say it all the time, especially at the gay bar.

I was now officially gay. I told all of my old friends

I ran across and now all my co-workers knew, but I wasn't ready to tell my family yet, so I was leading this secret life that consisted of being gay, and using drugs and alcohol.

I had completely transformed myself to the things of this world, and now I was in another prison, a stronghold stronger than drugs, stronger than alcohol. In fact, the Bible says in Matthew 17:21 (NKJV), *"However, this kind does not go out except by prayer and fasting."*

I have overcome a lot in my lifetime, by the mercy, grace, power, and answered prayers prayed by many Saints, especially my ancestors. I will say without a shadow of a doubt, sexual perversion and homosexuality had a much stronger hold on me than shooting drugs and alcohol ever did. I had to be loosed and completely delivered to come out of that sin and I am still walking it out. It is definitely a process. It was who I had become. My identity was all wrapped up in being gay. Being gay for me was just as real as me being black. I had believed every lie the enemy had told me. I had always been this way even as a child. The enemy was telling me lies as a child, whispering things in my ear, until finally many years later I believed it enough to act on it and I never turned back. It was something I was proud to be. I gained some sort of acceptance from being gay — acceptance I had been looking for my entire life.

It was a trap that had been set for me, waiting for years. I just didn't have the spiritual weapons I have now to fight back. Instead I fell and I fell very deep. There are many who never make it out. The only power strong enough to defeat this satanic power is Jesus. He is the Way, the Truth, and the Life.

The Word is power. It's the gospel that saves us through Jesus. I didn't know any scripture. In fact, at that time in my life, I couldn't pray myself out of a paper bag if my life depended on it.

John 14:6 says that the Father (God, as revealed in Jesus) is only known through Jesus. The verse says that this truth, this way to life, is a revelation by the Spirit of God that Jesus has identified as the way of forgiveness and redemption — wisdom or knowledge that will save people who are lost or guilty and weighed down with sin. The only One who can set us free from this prison and bondage is Jesus.

John 8:36 (NIV) says, *"So if the Son sets you free, you will be free indeed."*

That is my mission in life, to bring as many people as I can to Jesus because I found the way out. I searched and struggled, wandering in this "wilderness" of life for 35 of my 40 years, and Jesus grabbed my hand and led me out of myself and my misery to find him on this beautiful, joyous path towards the kingdom of God. He had chosen for me this before the foundations of the earth were formed. Before He formed me in my mother's womb, He knew me. I am so glad He chose to save me. He had the key to my heart, the key to unlock the prisons I was caged in for so many years. He has now set me free and given me the keys to his children to unlock the keys to their hearts and pull them out of the same bondages that had me bound. He has anointed me to go back into the wilderness to those He has chosen to let loose, to set free and to bring them out of darkness into the light.

He has given me power over all of the shackles that needed to be broken, strongholds that had me bound, the things my flesh desired and craved for years for things I couldn't let go of. The hold it had on me left me completely powerless. Now He has given me the power to be able to stand up against every temptation this world has to offer. I could not reject alcohol. My body craved it. I could not reject drugs my flesh had been dependent on for so many years.

The desire to be with a woman, to fall in love and get married, living happily ever after – this was the picture I painted mentally, and the reality I believed I was living. I believed it with all my heart. When anyone would ask me what God thought about it, I replied, "Me and God have an understanding. He knows I'm gay. I will stand in front of Him one day and plead my case. He will accept me for who I am."

That was a lie straight from the pit of hell and the farthest thing from the truth.

The Bible clearly states in 1 Corinthians 6:9-11 (NKJV), *"Do you not know that the unrighteous will not inherit the kingdom of God? Do not be deceived. Neither fornicators, nor idolaters, nor adulterers, nor homosexuals, nor sodomites, nor thieves, nor covetous, nor drunkards, nor revilers, nor extortioners will inherit the kingdom of God. And such were some of you. But you were washed, but you were sanctified, but you were justified in the name of the Lord Jesus and by the Spirit of our God."*

I was one like that, but now I am right with God. I was a slave to all of those things I desired. I had to have them.

Aimee was a fleshly desire that I had to have. I felt I was in love with her. But lust is not love. I couldn't tell the difference between the two. To be honest I never knew what love was until I met Jesus. Now looking back, He had given me a true revelation that the love I had in my heart wasn't pure; it was tainted. The love of this world is not real love. It is a combination of feelings and emotions that our minds and soul are in control. My mind was controlling my flesh; therefore, my heart was controlled by my way of thinking. Clearly the power that was over me was darkness. I was nowhere near the light and the path I had been walking on was not the one God had for me. I was going the wrong way, and over the years I took a lot of people with me. Unknowingly, I caused them to stumble and God has forgiven me for that. He is such a good Father.

Aimee and I continued to drink and spend time together. I was falling deeper and deeper in love, all the while flirting with every pretty girl I could get my hands on. This whole gay thing had me going full speed ahead. Then the unthinkable happened. Aimee went to visit her family in Madison and winded up getting pregnant by a guy she was in love with. What the heck?! My heart was broken. She left me, going home to start her family and live happily ever after. I'm sure that was the plan. I started getting so drunk, I passed out every time I went out. Olga had to carry me out of the bar and sometimes help me crawl through my side window, because I didn't want my mom to see me belligerent.

I was hanging out with another girl who worked at Golden Corral. We hung out a lot. She had a boyfriend and would listen to my sad, sad story of Aimee breaking my heart. She knew her since we all worked and all hung out together, so she was well aware. It was pitiful really. Aimee was my first girlfriend and I wanted to marry her. It was a fact that I felt that way, but I was deceived, believing and living the lie was my reality.

I then met this girl that was older than I. Her name was Krista. She had beautiful long brown hair and was cute. I was clearly trying to get over Aimee, so I slept with her and we hung out a few times. That was the extent of our relationship. I started getting high again. I had quit for a while and decided to go back to one of my best friends, Meth, so I got on a good one. I remember one Saturday night everyone was working, and we were making plans on what we were going to do for that night. I had the whole dining room to myself, which was awesome for a Saturday night, and an opportunity for me to make a lot of money. I was too high, evidently, because I couldn't handle it alone and management had to step in and bus my tables and refill drinks for me. So, at the end of the night I got fired.

Greg called me into the office and said, "Everybody likes you. I like you. I hate to do this, but I have to fire you. If you can't handle a full dining room on a Saturday night you don't need to be a server here."

So, I walked out of that office feeling rejected and embarrassed. My life as I knew it was over. Here it was again, something I knew very well and just couldn't seem to hide from — failure. That spirit followed me my entire life — that is, until God set me free.

10

CHAPTER 10

Another Chapter In My Life

I was living with Trisha in Carriage House Apartments in the year 2000. She had just had Morgan. We weren't sober but we were not doing drugs at the time. Chasity had gotten me a job at Vanguard Answering Service. I had been there for about eight months. I had favor at this time from the owners of Vanguard. One Friday night, I was working second shift and everyone decided to leave. First shift is always supposed to wait until second shift shows up and relieves you from your position, otherwise all the calls will go to one person because there is no one else in rotation. That specific day the first shift supervisor and everyone working had to leave at exactly 4 p.m. Roanna, the supervisor, decided to take a chance and leave so I was the only one in rotation for hours. I was getting so many calls I had to put everyone on hold, and the wait times for businesses were over the top. I love an adrenaline rush. That's exactly what was going on. I was loving the excitement in that moment and I was doing everything I could to stay in the game. So, the owners of Vanguard called in and realized I was the only one who stayed and decided not to let everything fall apart and save the day. From that day on, the owners had a very high level of respect for me. This was definitely job security for me. I love being in the fire. I know I can handle it. The boss's wife, Linda, ended up catching a whiff of the entire situation and commended me for handling the situation on my own. I pretty much saved the company and they were pleased with my dedication.

That moment was short-lived and the trap the enemy had set for me was already in motion. Trisha came around and decided she wanted to work at Vanguard as well, so with Chasity and I vouching for her, she started immediately. The very first day she came in she was high and I asked her if she had any more. She said, "I have an endless supply. My dude is the dope man." We went and got high on break and continued to do that every single day afterwards. I was just getting started and she was already in full-blown addiction shooting up. She was wearing bandages on her hands, covering up her track marks, and I was getting free dope. We made a perfect match.

I was up for days at a time. Trisha and I were working together and getting high together. I was staying at her and Ed's trailer on the west side. Ed lived with his dad and his dad didn't mind us being there. He was glad to be around a couple of younger women. I would always hang out in the living room with him and just keep him company. His dad was retired and hardly ever left the house. He drank beer just about every day, so I would crack a few with him. I had it made — free dope, free beer, and a place to chill.

I remember the first time I shot up. I had been up for five days and we had just returned from the club. I was on the verge of passing out.

They were saying, "Let's get high."

I said, "There ain't enough dope in the world that can keep me up."

Ed said, "I bet if you do a shot, you would get up real quick."

I said, "No way!"

I remember him giving me a shot and the first word that came out of my mouth was, "Woah!"

I was sparked and high as a kite. I remember I was so high my eyes kept blinking and I told Trisha. She said, "That's because your tweeking."

They were laughing at me because I was so high. She tried to put a rag around my neck to help me out. Then all I remember was that I couldn't stop talking. I was talking about everything under the sun. I don't think I had ever been that high. Shooting meth takes you to a whole other level.

It was Mother's Day that morning. The last thing on my mind was calling Mom on Mother's Day. That day was the beginning of me going to a whole other level of addiction and we were on one for real. We ended up on a binge for months. I was participating in some very highly illegal activities that could have put me in prison for a very long time. I wasn't out to hurt anyone or make money, I was simply trying to get high and stay high. I always felt completely invincible when I was on meth. I never thought about the consequences of my actions. But the Lord had protected me through it all. Even then the Lord had His hand on me. Everyone around me would eventually disappear and get busted. At those times, by the grace of God, He would send me home.

I remember being on a three or four month binge, and I would hear the Holy Spirit tell me, " It's time to go home." I listened and went to my mother's house, took a shower, ate, and crashed for a few days. Every single time while I was home recuperating, I would get back up ready to go again and the crew I was running with all got busted. This happened to me all throughout the years I lived in the drug world. I knew it was the grace of God. My mother and grandparents were praying for me and the Lord answered their prayers.

I eventually lost my job at Vanguard. I just quit showing up because I was too strung out to function. Trisha was also fired. By that time they all knew we were doing the same thing, so I chose to save face. That journey was finally over when Ed, Trisha's boyfriend, got busted and sent to prison for cooking meth. I then went back home to my mother's house.

THE END FROM THE BEGINNING

CHAPTER 11

Back At My Mom's House

It was the same story. I got myself back together enough just to fall again. I was still in deep depression and I no longer had any income coming in. I was really desperate. My sister invited me to come to Henderson to live with her and her husband at the time, Jason. Jason had an older brother named Jeremy. We all used to get high together when Jason and Jeremy lived with their parents in Henderson. I remember getting extremely drunk off of whiskey. I believe we had a couple fifths of E&J and I was taking straight shots. I would get as drunk as I possibly could. I remember Jeremy, Jason's brother, coming over. I was laying down in the bed because I had drunk way too much. Jeremy came in as well, three sheets to the wind. I remember he came in there to talk to me. He had always liked me and asked me out a few times but I told him I was gay and didn't date men anymore. Soon he came into the bedroom and we were both highly intoxicated. Before you knew it we were having sex. It seemed like it lasted five seconds. I barely even remember it. I do remember him acting like his hip went out and that was the end of it. I went to sleep. That's all it took was five seconds.

Five seconds changed my entire life, because in that five seconds I got pregnant. I didn't even feel like anything happened, and neither did he. A few months later I started feeling very depressed and sick all the time. I lived with my mother in Evansville. We were now living in a tiny two-bedroom apartment. Mom was really struggling at the time financially and emotionally. I was sitting in the living room talking on the phone to my sister telling her how horrible I felt and she said she thought I was pregnant. Ashley at that time had two children so I believed her when she said that. Something in my spirit agreed. I got off the phone with my sister, knocked on my mother's door, and told her, "Ashley thinks I'm pregnant."

What a way to start a conversation.

I was scared and ashamed. I couldn't even take care of myself. I was living with my mother, jobless, and the last thing that I was ready for was to have a baby. I was still in and out of addiction. I slept most of the days away, being depressed. I already knew what I was going to do. There was no doubt in my mind. I was going to get an abortion.

My mother then asked me, "Who is the father?"

I replied, "Jason's brother, Jeremy."

I then shut my door and we didn't speak of it until I told her I was going to Illinois to the doctor to get an abortion. I had my mind made up, and I didn't even feel guilty about it. I felt in my heart I was doing the right thing for everyone. To me it wasn't even fair. I didn't choose to purposely get pregnant. This was not something I even thought about doing, but the deed was done.

I told myself, "You're an alcoholic, a drug addict and you have nothing to offer a child. I sure wouldn't want a mom like me."

I called Jeremy and told him I made an appointment and he had to pay for it, so he drove me the two hours away. We got a hotel room for the night and I made an appointment the following morning.

There were people standing outside of the clinic, holding signs and shouting. It really didn't bother me. I was just ready to hurry up and get everything over with. Once I left, I actually felt relieved. I don't remember even really feeling those emotions until years later. I was used to suppressing and numbing myself. There were a lot of feelings, hurts, painful situations I had pressed deep down and didn't ever let them come up and that was one of them. After that, I never spoke with Jeremy again. There were no hard feelings. I still thought of him as a buddy but there was just no relationship or friendship ever really established.

Olga and I went to the Time Out Lounge one night. I had gotten back in touch with her and wanted to just go out and have a good time and get back to the old me, the Kristin that had some joy and loved to smile. When I wasn't in a pit of depression, I was a happy person, very personable, and a people person. I treated people the way I wanted to be treated, with respect, and exceptionally and genuinely nice. I came across this really cute blond and I was trying to spit some game on her. Why not?

Well, this really cute blonde turned out to be Erin Rickabaugh. I knew her from back in the day. She used to come over to my house when me and Chasity lived on Florida Street. Erin and Chasity had grown up together as children. I knew a little about what Erin was about. You know what they say birds of the same feather flock together. She was there by herself and was happy to see me. We had a couple drinks and talked and she invited me over to her house after the club. I knew one or two things were going to happen. Either we were going to hook up or she had the hookup.

I know the game well enough to know, no one is going to invite you over to their house at 3:30 a.m. after the club unless sex or drugs are a part of the plan. She said something about her boyfriend being at the house, so that let me know we were going to be doing some drugs. Of course, I was correct. We ended up doing some hot rails of meth and smoking all night long.

From that day on we kicked it 24/7. We became the best of friends. Erin was a single mother with a son. At that time he was eight or nine years old. She was my road dog for sure. She had a good job as a phlebotomist, her own trailer, a license, a car, and she was responsible. Mom allowed her to come and pick me up and she was dependable. She needed a friend just as much as I did, and we both liked to party really hard. She had access and the dope man was her best friend, so the supply was plentiful. Erin loved men just as much as I loved women, so we never crossed that line. We were in sexual situations together but we never dated. Erin and I hung out for years. She was selling just as much as she was doing them. I was just the middle-man most times. I was in it because I was an addict, doing whatever it took to get high. I was the person who knew how to get any drug you wanted or knew someone who did, so I just hooked people up with the right people and for that I got free dope. I stayed at her trailer with her and Levi more than I did my mother's house.

Erin always had money so she would have to pay my way in the club. I would hustle up drinks from men, so by the end of the night I was beyond lit. Then we would go hang out with some of her guy friends or the man she was seeing at the time. We would stay up all night, smoking dope and drinking beer. Erin and I were two of a kind. I helped her find clients to sell to so I could continue to reap the benefits of getting high for free. We were just having fun.

I had finally gotten a job at a steak house waiting tables. At this time, I was able to function and maintain just enough to be able to hold a job. I lived with my mother at Brentwood, the same townhouses we lived in when we first moved to Evansville.

Bre and Erica were in high school at the time and I lived at Mom's. I could walk back and forth to work. I was just living life day to day off of the tips that I made at work, enough to party and support my many habits. Mom would need help from time to time for my sisters. They played basketball and needed money for uniforms, basketball shoes, and books for school. I would help as much as I could, which wasn't near enough of what she needed while taking care of us all and providing a roof over our heads.

Then to my surprise here came Krista P., an old friend I came across again from the past. We had hooked up once before, while I was working at Golden Corral. Here she was again. It is always easier to reacquaint yourself with someone you already have established a relationship with before, whether it's sexual or drugs. In this case it was both. It took a minute for us to click, but we clicked.

The relationship we had before was destructive. The friendship we were forming was headed down the road of destruction as well. I already had previous feelings she had no clue about. That immediately rose to the surface as soon as I saw her for the first time. I do remember asking her if she wanted to do some meth and she was game, so from that day forward we were always hanging out getting high and working together. There wasn't a waking moment we weren't together, which made it easier for me to fall for her, and that I did. I fell in love with her and she definitely provoked everything that I did, which played a huge part in my mixed emotions. The fact that we had an intimate encounter really didn't help things.

She became the number one person in my life. I did everything I possibly could to make her happy. Anything I had was hers and that went both ways.

We were both using opiates, meth, alcohol, at a very high level, barely even functioning. She had also been on methadone, so our life consisted on making money to do drugs and going to hell and back to get them.

Morals and values were completely out of the equation. Getting high and staying high was our daily routine.

I lived with my mother and she about had it with my lifestyle and the choices I was making. At this point, I was draining her emotionally and financially. Her hair and her eyebrows were falling out and I asked her why.

She explained, "Because of you," implying I was stressing her out.

Apparently, when she went to the doctor, he confirmed that was the reason.

I had lost so much weight. I was used to being 145-150. I now weighed 113. I thought I was looking good. The truth is I lost so much weight because I was so strung out.

I went to work one day and my managers called me in the office and just wanted me to know from a friend's perspective that I was too skinny and I really needed to lay off of the drugs. These were actually the same people who I got high with and they were telling me that my slip was showing. In other words, you could see the monkey on my back and I couldn't hide my addiction from anyone.

I was still hanging out with Erin. She was actually the one selling it to me and all the women I was getting high with.

Erin now had a new boyfriend. He was nothing like Chris. He didn't do meth. He had a really quiet personality and he had a good job. He smoked weed. That was the common ground him and Erin met on. He moved in with her. All Erin really wanted was to be a family. All she knew was how to be dysfunctional and the addictive personality that she carried reflected in every aspect of her life. That was the common ground we stood on.

Krista was just like Erin. She was addicted to men and drugs. Her family life was also broken. Her parents couldn't hardly handle her behavior, which created drama, and her family couldn't stand me because I was gay and me and Krista were drug buddies.

Looking back, I wouldn't want my daughter hanging with me either. I wasn't about the right thing and I was walking in darkness and leading the way. That's where my mother picked up the concept of "the blind leading the blind," which is also biblical. This appears several times in the Bible with similar stories appearing in the gospels of Matthew, Luke, and Thomas.

"Every plant that my heavenly Father has not planted will be pulled up by the roots. Leave them; they are blind guides {of the blind}." (Matthew 15:13-14a, NIV).

Krista was a very manipulative person and used every person who was around her to get what she wanted. The feelings I had for her were very distorted. I was again in a relationship all by myself with the hope and intentions of us being in a relationship. She was in a sexual relationship with everyone around her, so we all had expectations on her, whether it was sexual or, in my case, emotional.

There came a season where we were just too radical to even function. We both ended up losing our jobs. She got really sick from not going to the methadone clinic, and I slept for a week straight and quit doing all the meth I was doing. Finally, that friendship ended and all the hurtful things she had done I didn't see before came to the surface. God put a wedge in between us and I was able to move on. On to the next one.

CHAPTER 12

Lonely Road Of Destruction

I got myself back together just enough to get myself in another trap the enemy had set for me. I just couldn't break loose for anything in the world. That was just it; I was looking for answers and comfort from the counterfeit things in this world — alcohol, drugs, and sex, disguising themselves as peace and joy, which always turned into disaster on a lonely road of destruction.

True peace and joy only come from the Lord. Those are the beatitudes which teach that people are blessed even during trials and tribulations that create storms in life. The beauty of it is we will receive eternity in heaven. We are blessed in having honorable qualities such as being pure, meek, merciful, and walking the earth as peacemakers. Living a righteous life full of unspeakable joy and peace that surpasses all understanding that only comes from walking down the path of righteousness with God, accepting His son Jesus as a sacrifice for the sins of all.

I walked this earth poor in spirit for 35 of my 40 years. I now wake up every morning looking forward to what God has for me and anticipating all the promises and blessings He has given me, because my heart is right with God. I have decided to follow Jesus, which is so much easier than the drama, chaos and struggles that came from the road I was on.

The Word says in Matthew 11:30 (NIV), *"For my yoke is easy and my burden is light."*

We come unto Him and we shall find rest unto our souls. I now have that rest.

So, I had just got back on track to a certain extent and started working at CRF again. I had worked there off and on starting at the age of 20. I was now 27. I lived with Mom. Erin had just gone to jail. She got caught on a dealing charge. That day she was being shady with her boyfriend, but I was nowhere around. There was a girl I worked with at CRF previously, Caprice, who I used to get high with. I introduced Erin and Caprice. Anyway, Caprice wore a wire on Erin that day and set her up. Erin went to the Vanderburgh County Jail to visit her mom and never came out.

I then had no choice but to slow down, and once again everyone around me went to jail. I had just got a promotion at CRF for Team Leader and I was actually taking my job seriously and working really hard to try to finally succeed and break through the prison that had me bound all these years. I wanted to be loosed. I wanted to live a good life and be a good person and just be happy. All I had known was living from paycheck to paycheck, and alcoholism ran rampant in my family, so I was doing good if that was the only substance that I was using.

I tried to read the Bible and live the right way, but homosexuality and addiction was a barrier I just didn't have the power to get past or find a way through. One day Zeke, Erin's boyfriend at the time, came in work to drop me off a pack of cigarettes. He and I had become really close friends. We spent a lot of time together. We all practically lived together, so when Erin went to jail, we looked out for each other. We were both hurting. We both loved Erin, his girlfriend and my best friend.

I got paid that Friday. I had been working and living with Mom. I gave Zeke some money to pay the lot fee for Erin's trailer that we all stayed in. Becca saw Zeke and asked me if that was my husband. My sister blurted out, "My sister is a lesbian."

Becca told her that her mom was a lesbian. From that moment on Becca was feeling me on a level other than just co-workers or friends. That was the moment she said she was first attracted to me. I had no clue.

I also had no intentions of even thinking about a married woman with kids in any inappropriate way. I had morals and values that I stood on and that was one of them. Addiction will take you places you said you would never go. Addiction will have you doing things you never dreamt you were even capable of doing.

My sister, Ashley, would ride back and forth to work with Becca so I caught a ride with them. I offered Becca gas money and let her know I appreciated her giving us a ride home. I made it clear I wasn't the kind of person who would take advantage of someone. It was a different story with Ashley. Ashley was doing pills but she wasn't drinking alcohol, so she believed the lie that she was sober. She was attending A.A. classes with Davy so she thought I was a bad influence.

I remember Rebecca saying that her and her husband, Aaron, were throwing a shindig at her house in Henderson. Ashley told her not to invite me because I was an alcoholic and she and Davy didn't want to be around me. Becca told me what she said. I had no intentions of going, but the simple fact that Ashley told that to my team which I was manager over was belittling to me.

I told my mom about it. She put Ashley in check and told her never to throw someone under the bus, especially her family. Mom reminded her she wasn't better than anyone.

Ashley and I hardly ever got along unless we were teaming up to get hold of drugs. Other than that, we could never seem to find any common ground.

I remember like it was yesterday. I was at work and was working overtime on a Friday night. Becca asked me if I wanted to go to lunch with her and I said, " I'm broke." She replied, "I'll buy," with that thick country twang Becca had, which was adorable. I agreed to dinner. Then on lunch we hopped in her blue Kia sport. We went to McDonald's drive-through and brought our food back to work. I assumed we were going inside to eat, but she insisted we eat in her truck together. I felt weird. Why would she want to sit outside with me? What are we going to do, listen to music? She then started to share an experience she had as a young girl which was completely innocent, and she asked me if that meant she was gay.

I started laughing and said, "No, that doesn't mean you're gay," in a very calm and monotone voice.

Then she said, "I'm attracted to you, Kristin."

I didn't even think about it as I blurted out, "I'm attracted to you, too."

There was a weird silence that came after that and I said, "Okay, let's go in now," feeling awkward and very uncomfortable.

So, I went in thinking, "What in the world just happened?"

Becca was thinking, "Okay, now me and Kristin are in a relationship."

She gave me a ride home and gave me a love letter that she wrote to me right after we had our little weird conversation.

I knew then I was in trouble.

New Year's Eve was now here and I had no money, no plans, and I needed a beer really bad. So, I called Becca in desperation. There was two feet of snow outside and I had no ride. She offered my sister, Erica, $25 to take me to the riverboat with her and her husband Aaron. I thought I was just going to go party with them. Becca was on a whole other level. She just wanted to be with me. So, we had drinks and just talked as her husband kept giving her money for us to gamble. We were having a ball. Then I pulled one of my signature moves. She was in the bathroom and I went in her stall, locked the door, threw her up against the bathroom wall and kissed her. I'm not sure what led me to do that, but I know the alcohol had some say-so and I was having fun with her, so there it went.

That was the moment I crossed the line and our friendship became a relationship. She mentioned later that was a moment she knew we were going to be together, plus she was convinced whoever you spend New Year's with is who you will be with the whole year. She had already fallen for me. I could never figure out how or why. Her husband was a good provider. She didn't even have to work. All she did most of the time was shop. She was just working at CRF because she was bored and she liked to have extra money. She was a stay-at-home mom and she wanted to get out of the house. Becca was 25 years old and never really got to have any fun. She didn't do the whole party thing because she had kids, so she had a lot of fun with me. That was one thing I was really good at — having a good time.

So, we had drinks at the riverboat all night long and, rather than them drop me off at home, we went back to Becca and Aaron's house. Aaron was hanging with one of his buddies, and Becca and I were kicking it, so it wasn't like we were alone together. We got to Henderson and Aaron and his buddy went to get more alcohol from his buddy's house so we could stay up and play cards. Becca's kids were at their grandparents for the night, so as soon as Aaron and his friend left she mentioned the kiss in the bathroom that occurred earlier when we were on the riverboat. She said she liked it.

I said, "I'll do it again if you want me to," so I did, and we had our first sexual encounter that night on the couch.

Aaron and his friend came back. We were sitting out in the garage smoking cigarettes, falling in love with each other for the first time. I was not even for a moment physically attracted to her until that night, but as far as being in a relationship, I was used to women just wanting to have sex with me and keep it a secret with no intentions on being in a relationship with me.

I was just going to take it for what I thought it was. I had been used to women wanting to hide being gay or bi-sexual. I assumed this was the exact same thing. So we all were playing cards and Aaron was teaching me how to play poker. Becca was too busy trying to rub her feet up against mine under the table. I couldn't focus on the card game and I was three sheets to the wind, so I was just going with the flow.

The next morning, I was passed out on the couch and Rebecca came up to kiss me on the forehead before anyone was awake. I had no idea until she told me. She said I smelled like beer and all she wanted to do was kiss me. She loved the smell of beer on my breath and the taste reminded her of her dad who passed away years before. So, my flaws were the things she loved about me. I couldn't understand the reasoning behind it, but it worked out to my advantage. That's why the fact that I was a heavy drinker didn't bother her — because her dad had drank. I woke her and the youngest baby, Riley, who was one year old at the time. We all got in the truck. She asked me if I regretted what we did the night before. I told her no; I then asked her if she regretted it.

She replied, "No, we can do it again if you want to."

I started laughing and said, "Okay."

We were both going into work. We had a few hours to make up, so we were going to see each other again that day.

I had a horrible hangover so I went home and laid down for an hour or so. I took my phone off the hook. We had land lines then. She had been calling me non-stop waiting for me to come in as soon as I hit the door. She had already written me a love letter. I was like, "Wow! I'm usually the one who is sweating some chick and she is already sweating me."

It actually felt good to have the upper hand. Not only that but just feeling wanted. Falling in love was not even on my agenda. I just thought this was a hookup thing and she was acting like this was more than that. I'm usually the one who falls first but I had no intentions of falling for her, especially with her being married. I already had a wall built and my heart was guarded.

Something happened. She was catching serious feelings and I was just going with the flow.

We started spending a lot of time together. We worked together and I would go stay the weekends with her. Aaron worked nights so we were all alone with the kids and our relationship got serious fast. I loved the fact that Becca just adored me. It was obvious she was in love and I seriously didn't know what to do with that. She bought me a cellphone and bought me everything voluntarily. I wasn't used to that but that was her love language and she took just as good of care of me as she did her kids. For that I fell in love with her. All I remember is after a couple months of dating we were so in love she wanted to get a divorce from Aaron. We were going to get married. I loved her kids. She had a boy and three girls, ages 10, 8, 2 and 1.

She came up with the notion that me and Erica should get our own place and we could be able to spend more time together. I agreed and me and Erica moved out of our mom's and got an apartment at Hornbrook. They were really nice townhomes. They were right down the street from where I worked so it was also more convenient for our relationship. I could walk to work if I needed to. Erica had a part-time job at the University of Southern Indiana and also went to school there, so we were going to split the bills. Becca bought almost everything we needed to decorate the apartment and her and the kids came over all the time. She was to the point where she was no longer sexually involved with her husband, and that was causing problems between them. I told her I didn't want her making love to anyone but me. We were crazy about each other and Aaron was starting to get jealous. I wasn't really sure what to do about the situation. All I knew was I loved Becca and we were getting married.

It was during this time that I started taking Adderall. I would take one before work. Both Becca and I started taking them on Friday and Saturday nights so we could stay up all night together, loving on each other, talking and making plans for our future.

I always asked Becca, "Why me? Aaron is a good man. He is a good father and a good provider. You don't even have to work."

The money she was spending on me was only because Aaron took care of the bills and she spent her money on me. I was the type of person who didn't take advantage of people and I felt bad for Aaron.

Sometimes Becca and I would be laying in their bed and I felt some conviction, but she obviously didn't care so I just followed her lead. She explained to me over and over again, "I love Aaron but I'm in love with you Kristin and I want a life with you. I want to be with you forever."

That's all it took for me. After hearing it several times I convinced myself she was the one for me and for the first time in four months I let myself fall in love with her and the idea that we were going to be a family. Her kids absolutely loved me and I absolutely loved them back. She used to tell me all the time that the youngest baby was mine. I would just bust up laughing because all of her children had blond hair and blue eyes.

We were quite the couple. My family loved Becca. Even my mother couldn't help noticing the change in me. I was working and being more responsible than she had seen me be in a long time. She was just happy I wasn't on drugs anymore.

Everyone at work knew we were together and accepted our relationship. The only people who didn't know were her family and Aaron, but all that was about to change very soon.

I just let Becca do whatever she felt like she needed to do and handle things the way she felt they needed to be handled. In the beginning I had the reins and I was running the show as far as who was in complete control of how far this relationship was going to go, but the tables had turned and Becca was now running the show.

I thought, "Well, she loves me, so I'll do anything I can to make her happy."

From that moment on all I wanted to do was love her as much as she loved me and to spend the rest of my life making her happy. The fact that she was married didn't even matter to me anymore. Our relationship had gone to a whole other level and she was planning on getting a divorce. If that was what she wanted then that's what she was going to do.

I remember she was helping me and Erica move into our apartment. It was after work on a Friday around 8 p.m. Aaron was in Henderson with the kids. Becca and I had just come out of my bedroom walking down the hallway and my niece, Ellie, Ashley's daughter, was in the living room. As we were walking down the hallway someone was lightly knocking on the door. Ellie was in the living room and asked who it was. Becca's mom was at the door and had driven all the way from Morton's Gap, Kentucky unannounced. Ellie was around eight years old and all she heard was, "It's just Becca's mom."

She was trying to get Ellie to open the door. Her mom was with her girlfriend, Holly. Becca's mom and Holly were together when Becca was a child, and her mother and father were still married. Becca's mom had an affair with a woman and now Becca was doing the same exact thing. Becca's mom came in with Holly, irate, and asked her what in the hell she was doing.

Becca said, "I'm helping Kristin move," which she was, but we sure were taking our time. Ellie took off in one of the back bedrooms crying because she realized she wasn't supposed to have let anyone in the apartment.

Becca's mom asked me, "Are you in love with my daughter?"

I said yes. I felt as if I had to tell the truth. I couldn't just lie to her mother's face. She went to slap the daylights out of me but Becca jumped in front of me and took the hit. All I remember was saying, "Whoa, whoa, whoa…" I was shocked. This was some Jerry Springer stuff going down, right in the middle of my living room.

Becca said to her mother, "She didn't do anything."

This was all Becca. I was the one who was gay but she was the one who initiated the whole thing. She was the one who came on to me and convinced me to be with her.

I wasn't trying to break up a happy home, but like my boss at the time, Lisa Messina, told me, "That home wasn't happy or you wouldn't have been able to break it up."

So, Becca and her mother finally exited the premises and, on their way out, Becca's mother told her clearly, "You ain't gonna be with no n....."

Yes, she said the "N" word.

It wasn't even the fact that I was a woman or that Becca was married. It was the principle that I was black and she was white.

I then asked Holly, her girlfriend, "Did she just say what I think she said?"

Holly replied, "Yes, she did."

I was like, "Wow, what have I gotten myself into?"

Becca and her mom sat out in the truck talking for over an hour. I called Becca's cell and asked her if everything was okay down there. She said yes. I never once disrespected her mother. I wasn't even mad at her for saying what she said. I understood how and why she was upset. She was just trying to protect Becca from the hurt and pain that was to come because she had already gone through it.

Becca told her she was going to apologize to me, that she loved me, and we were going to be together. She told her mom if she would not accept those conditions she would not be a part of her life anymore. So, from that moment on, I was convinced that Becca really did love me with her whole heart and we were going to be together forever.

Everything was starting to get harder. My sales percentages had decreased drastically, and my team's numbers were suffering as well. I had to get hold of this problem or there was a possibility I would be demoted or, worst case scenario, fired from my job. Things were slowly but surely starting to fall apart. I was not sure how to hold it all together. I remember having a team leader meeting and my boss letting me know something had to change. I had spent the night with Becca and I was driving Erin's Jeep to work that morning. I made a wrong exit turn which made me run around 20 minutes behind. I was supposed to be at work setting a good example for my team. Instead I was all about Becca trying to make her happy, writing love letters to her while I'm supposed to be focused on my job. I was really getting stressed and there was a lot of weight on my shoulders with bills and work.

As soon as I walked in, I was asked to join my bosses and Joanie the hiring manager (who absolutely loved me). They were getting ready to let me go. I was called in there to be fired. I remember I started crying and I asked Joanie to go and get Becca's keys so I could avoid the humiliation of being fired. I ran out of that office crying like a baby, trying to figure out what was happening in my life and why everything was starting to fall apart. I drove her truck to the liquor store and got really drunk, then laid down to take a nap. She kept calling me to make sure I was okay. I was starting to get depressed. How was I going to pay my rent now? Erica could barely pay the light bill, and Becca couldn't afford to pay $650 a month. The only thing now was to wait for an eviction if I didn't figure out how to come up with rent money.

We began making plans to move to Kentucky with her family and started making trips to visit. She inherited a house in Morton's Gap. It was her father's house and he left it to Becca. I was going to her mom's house visiting her family. Her mother lived in a trailer with Holly. Holly had told Becca that they slept in separate bedrooms. God told her she was going to go to hell if she continued to be in a relationship with Becca's mom. That part Becca didn't share with me until much later.

Becca ended up getting us a house in Morton's Gap rather than living in her father's house. While Aaron was at work one evening, we rented a U-Haul and got her furniture and moved in our house together. Becca's mom and Holly had gotten to know me and realized I did love Becca and her children and really had her best interest at heart. I had been saying I was ready to settle down and have a family and Becca and the kids were now my family. Erica moved in with me and was planning on getting a part-time job and going to the university that was in Kentucky.

Becca and I had planned on working at Tyson with Holly. She said she was going to get us both a job there and that was our happily-ever-after.

I remember asking her, "You would rather shovel poop and be with me than be with Aaron, when you don't even have to work? I don't think you are sure of what you want!"

She told me, "Don't tell me what I want. I know what I want, and I want you."

That was the first argument we had which made me love her even more if that was possible. The work of the enemy is so fierce. I was deceived in such a way I really thought this was true love. I felt in my heart that she was the one for me, and all along I had fallen into a trap of sexual perversion and didn't even recognize it. Becca was also deceived. The love that she had for me was an illusion the enemy had placed in her mind that led her to leave her husband and that's what she planned on doing.

I have to admit, I never met a woman who spoiled me and took as good of care of me as she did. She did everything for me. When she got off work early, she would go by my apartment and clean it for me. She always left love letters on my bed. She decorated my entire apartment. Her and the kids would come over every weekend. Aaron was starting to wonder why she was spending so much time with me. He didn't like it. By then it was too late. I already had her heart and she had mine.

So, we were moving to Morton's Gap. I remember my last night in my apartment I was having second thoughts and I knew things were going to be completely different. I was going to have a wife and kids to be responsible for.

I couldn't even take care of myself. How was I going to provide for them? I told myself that Becca was a very good mother and we complement each other, so together we can do anything. I meant every word of it, but that was not reality. That was another lie the enemy told me that I believed. The crap was about to hit the fan; we just couldn't see it yet. So, I went to sleep in my bed for the last time and realized I was in way too deep to back out now, plus I loved Becca. Why was I having second thoughts?

The next morning Erica and I rented a U-Haul and packed everything up and moved to Kentucky. My mom wasn't really happy about it. For one thing, she was going to miss us, and second, she knew that part of Kentucky we were moving to was known to be racist and there were no African-Americans who lived there. My mom had experienced a lot more as far as prejudice and racism than I had. She was born in the late '50s and I was born in 1980, so we had two totally different outlooks on these issues, even though they were issues that would always be.

I was still geeking on Adderall and was up for a few days as we were moving. Of course, my addictions were trying to creep back up on me and I was in no position to fight against it. I had lost my job, moved to Kentucky with the love of my life, and I still wasn't completely happy. I didn't have a state issued ID, so I knew I wasn't going to be able to start working until I got that taken care of, and I sure wasn't going to get anything done in a different state with no driver's license and no vehicle of my own. I was beginning to see how I was digging a deeper and deeper hole that I didn't have the tools to get out of.

Becca changed immediately. It was as if the moment we moved in with each other she became very controlling and very distant. It was like our relationship was already missing something. The closeness we once shared with each other, when she was all about me and always wanted to make sure I was happy, disappeared. I tried to get that back, but the harder I tried the more distant we became. I knew she was going through a divorce and that had to be the reason she was just being flat out mean and disrespectful. This wasn't the Becca I knew, the woman who would do anything for me, the woman who absolutely adored me. Now it seemed as if she despised me. My feelings were hurt and all I wanted was for us to be happy.

It was only a few weeks into the move this all came about. I couldn't wrap my mind around what was happening. She was working second shift at Tyson Foods and I was watching all four children during the day. Becca would come home right before the kids went to bed. I had been waiting for her to come home all day. I wasn't used to being responsible for taking care of four children, plus cooking and cleaning. I felt like Becca took Aaron's place working nights and I took Becca's place taking care of the kids. I was so overwhelmed, but this is what I wanted — a family of my own. She was acting a lot different than I was used to. The house would be spotless and the kids well taken care of, but she came in yelling at me for having the radio on while I was cleaning the kitchen.

While she was gone, I listened to James Morrison, "U Make it Real for Me, " and Alicia Keys "Like You'll Never See Me Again." Those were the songs we fell in love with. I remember I was driving me home one day before we started dating, and that song came on the radio. I loved that song by Alicia Keys. Becca and I turned it all the way up and sang the heck out of that song. It was raining and she said that was the night she realized she was into me because she was imagining I was singing that song to her. That was going to be our wedding song.

The only way I could keep my spirits up in the stressful situation I was now in, with the divorce going on between Becca and Aaron, was to remember the good times, the things that reminded me we were in love. I had to replay all the things that made me fall in love with her over and over again in my mind until I believed we were still in love, despite all the chaos and confusion and quality time I was not getting any more. I was holding on by a thin thread and she was acting a fool. She left me with the kids to go out and drink and play cards with her friends. I had no idea who they were, and the fact that now we were hiding our relationship from everyone when everyone in Evansville knew we were together really ticked me off. I was like, this is starting to feel like all the other relationships I was in that never worked out. We weren't talking any more, the love we used to have stayed in Indiana, and this was hell for me. I tried to tell myself all this too shall pass, but the reality was everything I had put Aaron through I was going through but 10 times worse.

You reap what you sow and all the hurt and pain I had put Aaron through I was now feeling. Everything she did to Aaron she was now doing to me. I was already experiencing the consequences I was going to have to pay for my actions — the wrath of God. When you mess with a marriage, a covenant made under God, the backlash is so unbearable. Nothing you do will prosper.

The loneliness I felt was immense — the rejection I was now experiencing from Becca. It's horrible when the shoe is on the other foot. Truth is, if I had the chance to do it all over again, I would have never taken a man's wife. But the love I had for her was so real; the lie the enemy told us both, we couldn't resist. I was lost — but now I'm found.

I was truly sorry, and I prayed for Aaron, asking the Lord to forgive me, which He has. I have also forgiven myself. If I would ever cross paths with Aaron, I would, from my whole heart, tell him that I love him as a brother in Christ, and I am sorry for the heartache and pain I caused him. He was a good man and was a good friend to me. He didn't deserve that.

I spent the next five years trying to get over Becca and the kids. God punished me for the evil I had done. We ended up losing our house in Morton's Gap. We moved into her mother's trailer. It was Becca's mom, Holly, me, Becca, and her four kids in a three-bedroom trailer. Becca was talking to other men, not coming home after work, leaving me with the kids all the time. I had no life, no job, no money. I was an alcoholic who lived in a dry county. Becca and I fought about beer almost daily. I needed something to ease the pain.

I had to numb myself somehow or another, and beer was my go-to. I would get up in the mornings, get the kids on the bus, watch the other two girls all day because they were too young for preschool and, as soon as the older two got off the bus, I would make them dinner, get ready for bed, and start all over again the next day. Becca was missing in action and blaming it all on work, but I knew exactly what was going on. Truth is she just didn't feel the same way about me as she did in the beginning. I believe the divorce changed her in a way she didn't even realize. I was still in love with her and still standing by her side through it all. Her mom and Holly actually grew to like and respect me. They knew I loved Becca and took as good care of the kids as I knew how.

I had really gotten close to the three-year-old. She was at the age where she would wake up in the morning and start calling my name. Becca used to play that role but somehow I was taking care of the kids all by myself. Holly worked at Tyson and Becca's mom was a care-giver, so it was just me and the kids. I would tuck the two youngest ones in every night. They would come up to me and say, "Kristin, time to go night-night." So, I would lay down with the kids until they fell asleep.

I couldn't take staying at that trailer every day and not working any more. I was getting so depressed I didn't even feel good about myself. I went from having it all — well, as good as I'd had it for a long time — to having absolutely nothing, and it was obvious I didn't have Becca anymore.

Our relationship was shipwrecked, so I decided to move back home to get a job, save some money, and we could meet somewhere in the middle. I was backed in a corner in Kentucky. I had to go to the license branch to get all the paperwork I should have had before I went to another state, trying to reestablish myself. Really, I was just setting myself up for failure. Our relationship failed.

I remember my mother telling me this, which was biblical, "You can't date someone else's wife and expect things to work out."

The Bible clearly refers to it: *"You shall not commit adultery."*

It is one of the Ten Commandments. Adultery is sexual relations in which at least one participant is married to someone else. According to the book of Genesis, marriage is a union established by God himself. I wouldn't wish the wrath that God places on the person who plays a part in it on my worst enemy. I went through hell and was in an unseen prison for many years from this experience, and more than one experience in sleeping with a married woman. A lot of the reasoning behind the drugs, alcohol, and suffering was a result of those sins. I was just looking for love in all the wrong places. The morals and values I once had now seemed to be in a grey area. Once you have crossed that line, there is no turning back.

I came back home and lived with my mother, heartbroken of course. I went to what I knew best, my old best friend, Meth. It didn't take, but one time and I was off and running. I ended up in Princeton with my dad for a week, smoking dope. I got myself together enough to get a job at a factory. I got my first paycheck and was feeling good about myself. I gave my mom some money, bought what I needed, and put $100 in the bank. But all it took was for Becca to call me up on the phone and tell me she loved me and she needed some money, so that $100 I had in the bank was wired to her the next day.

I was still crazy about her and wanted us to get it back together. I just wasn't ready or willing to give up on us. I couldn't stop loving her even if I tried. I was trapped and completely and totally infatuated with her. The thought of us not being together — I could just die. I couldn't tell the difference. Was it just infatuation or was it real love? Whatever it was, it had a hold on me. I couldn't let go.

Then the unthinkable happened. I started blowing up her phone. She wasn't returning any of my phone calls. I knew something was up. I started calling her on her job and then finally I got a hold of Holly at Tyson. She said she would have Becca call me and she did just that. Becca called me and said almost verbatim: "If I didn't have kids Kristin we would be together forever. I can't be in a gay relationship with you."

Story of my freakin' life.

This hadn't even been my idea. This was all her doing. She was the one who just had to be with me. I gave her plenty of opportunities to get out and she wouldn't. She was 100 percent sure we were getting married and were going to live happily ever after.

I tried to avoid what I knew one day would be my reality. She just ripped my freakin' heart out and there was nothing I could do to change her mind.

Or was there? I was bound and determined to mend what was broken. I just knew I could fix things. You have to get through the good, the bad, and the miserable times. I was a loyal person. I wasn't just going to let her go. You have to fight for love and I wasn't going out without a fight — at least that's what they say in the movies. If you know what you want, fight for it. These principles didn't particularly apply in this situation. That goes to show, we pick and choose the things we are willing to live by and the things we are not.

If my life had been based on biblical or even by good morals and values, I would not have even been in this situation. Being with a married woman clearly defied both. So, I tried to move on but clearly, I was an emotional wreck and the only thing I could think about is how much I missed my wife and my kids. I felt like I failed, our happily-ever-after was short lived. We didn't even make it a year before we wrecked both of our lives.

She was a lot worse off than she was when she started. She went from living in a beautiful suburban neighborhood with a husband who paid all the bills. She was more than well off and had it made. Now she was always broke, living in a small trailer, working in a factory without me, which was the whole reason she left that life in the first place. We both were walking out the consequences of our actions and I couldn't deal. I felt like I could kill myself.

Everywhere I went I was high or drunk or both, and all I talked about was how much I loved Becca and how I was completely lost without her. It was a pitiful mess. I was depressed and couldn't move past it. A whole year went by and I was still missing her and had not even thought about moving on.

I remember once, I was up for a few days and I came

to the conclusion I was going to do whatever it took to get her back. I came in my apartment and was so out of it I wasn't sure I was even in the right apartment. I called Becca, asking her to come and get me. It was a cry for help, and I was trying to manipulate myself close enough to her where I would try to win her back and make things right between us. That was my thought process, when really I was just putting myself right back into the situation. I should have run, but I didn't want to leave. I left thinking we were going to stay together and regroup.

She had moved into a trailer with a guy she was dating, but he left her and the kids in the trailer. She was in a bad spot and needed someone to help her take care of the kids. I was on the verge of a nervous breakdown coming down off dope. I thought everything would get better if I we could just figure out how to find our way back to when we were in love. She had been lying to me the whole time and had been in another relationship that had already ended. On top of that, she had been sleeping with my sister's ex-boyfriend who used to come over and hang out. He knew how much I loved her the whole time they were messing around. In fact, she had initiated the whole thing and was texting him saying the same things she used to say to me.

I was irate, heartbroken, and couldn't believe the person she had become. She was the only one I had been with since we met, and I couldn't even think about being close to anyone else. How could someone who loved you so much be able to just move on like that? I stayed up on Adderall and drank every alcoholic drink she had in the refrigerator. She didn't even drink before. Now she had a six-pack in the fridge. I was hurt even more than before. This wasn't doing me any good and quite frankly made things even worse. I told her I was going home that weekend, so she took me back to Indiana. On the way, we came to an agreement. She was going to move back in with her mom and Holly and she wanted me to come back and watch the kids while she worked. I couldn't see past us being a family again. All she wanted was for me to be the nanny.

What a joke. I didn't realize this until much later after I was already stuck and in the most uncomfortable situation I could ever imagine being in. I was back in Kentucky living with her and the kids and playing mommy number two, trying to win back her love. She was currently seeing a guy named Mike. I remember we were all at the trailer and he came over. He had no idea me and Becca were ever together. I knew she was dating him but I wasn't going to tell her secret even though it was killing me inside. I had to hold all this in. The kids loved me to pieces, so it was so hard to even be present in this situation I had absolutely no control over.

I remember my heart beating 100 miles a minute. This wave of anxiety came over me. I had asked Becca to pick me up a six pack of beer so I could go in the back room alone and sort this all out in my head. I needed a beer so bad. I had to numb this unbearable pain and all these feelings that made me just want to burst into tears. She told me she had forgotten to pick up my beer. We lived in a dry county and I was on the verge of freaking out. I went in the back bedroom and placed my hand over my head and began to cry. Becca came in and in the most serious, angry tone she had ever heard from me, I said, "Get out now!"

She replied, "How can you still have feelings for me?"

I said again, "Get the hell out of here!"

All I wanted was to be alone. I couldn't stand to look at her. The woman I once adored and loved with every fiber of my being had turned into a monster. She kept on hurting me. She clearly didn't love me anymore and had moved on several times since we were together. I then realized that it was really over. The love she once had for me now belonged to someone else. I had done this to myself. I am the one who put myself back in this situation. The pain I was feeling should have been over with. I should have already dealt the broken heart and the desire to be with her forever. The truth was I didn't know how to stop loving her. I couldn't let it go. My heart wouldn't let me.

I cried myself to sleep and woke up the next morning determined to push all those feelings deep down inside of me and act like all this never happened. It was too painful to walk through it. I decided to hide it in my heart and put it in the back of my mind, hoping and praying that all this would just go away. That's the only way I knew how to deal with problems. That's what I had done my entire life, which explains why I had to drink and do drugs. When any hurts from the past or present would start to rise up, I would reach for the closest substance I could get my hands on.

I took the kids to the store and left Becca and Mike there alone. The whole time I was gone I was imagining the worst. I knew Becca and how she operates. This would be the time she would sneak in and try to make love to the person she was with, which wasn't me anymore. That thought alone made me sick. I tried to enjoy the kids because I knew I was getting ready to make my exit. My time here was up. I couldn't take this anymore. This is what it took for me to begin the process of letting her go. She needed me there to watch the kids while she worked and she was using me for that alone. It took all this for me to see that.

We got back from the store and Becca was sitting in the same place she was when I left but I could tell by the look on her face she had just finished having sex with that man. She tried to play it off so I wouldn't notice but I knew her all too well. I knew all the tricks. She played them on me many times before. I kept my cool.

The next day, me, Becca, and the kids were headed

into town. One of Becca's girls had on some sunglasses, complaining how she couldn't see.

I busted up laughing and told her, "Well take off your sunglasses and maybe you could see something."

Becca started dying laughing and I was still rolling. Becca pulled out of the driveway and we were headed up the road and she said to me, "I never knew anybody who loved anyone as much as you loved me."

And I replied without hesitation saying what was on my heart, "I still love you like that!"

I meant it and she knew I did. She was lost for words and there was an awkward silence that seemed like forever. I knew if I was going to move back home, I had to do it secretly because she didn't want me to go. I was the only person who would watch her kids while she worked. If I left, then she would have to find a replacement. I called Erica and Bre while Becca was working and arranged for them to pick me up the following day.

When the time came, I told her I was leaving, that I wasn't happy, and I needed to start a life of my own without her. She didn't want a relationship, so I was just wasting my time.

She was furious and replied, "You're not going anywhere. I'm not giving you my phone and I'm not taking you."

I knew that was exactly what she was going to say. I told her that my sisters were already on their way.

So, I left and haven't spoken to her since.

13

CHAPTER 13

Short-lived Peace And Freedom

I felt this sense of peace and freedom I hadn't felt in a very long time. I was able to let her go and that's exactly what I did.

I was now 28 years old, moving back in with my mother. I just had one quick pit stop to make. As soon as I got back in town, I went to see my old buddy, Donnie. He lived off of Highway 41 and always had a way to get a hold of some dope. It was also a chill spot where I could go any time and have freedom to get high. If I needed a place to crash, take a shower, and just be on one, his spot was it.

I got pretty reckless when I came back. I went and bought a couple of Sudafed boxes and traded them for meth and started to get high again. The first people I contacted were Britney and Craig, Erin's sister and brother-in-law, my old drug buddies. I tried to smoke away all the hurt and pain I had experienced and was doing a pretty good job of it. I went back into the same old habits, same old meth-head. We were like family. If anyone of us was going through a major crisis in life, we would go to each other — broken, lost, broke — and we immediately knew what to do. Get high.

The beginning of my starting a new chapter in life consisted of me, Britney, and Craig. We were at a strip club on a Friday night and we had a few drinks in us. It was like 1 a.m. We decided we were going to scout out people in the club that may have drugs to sell or know how to get some. I remember seeing a young couple in their mid-20s, Chris and Charlie. I'm the one who scoped them out and said, "Do you know where to get some fire?"

They said, "We have some. You want to go try it?"

We were like, "For free?"

They said, "Yep."

So, we went out into their truck and smoked a bowl. It was good so we said, "Let's go chill and get high."

Britney and I were moving. We were ready to get up out of that club and go smoke some more dope.

We all drove to Craig and Britney's house over on Fares Avenue and bought a half and we all smoked. It was crazy because evidently Chris had been up for way too long. He locked himself in his truck accidently while passing out. A Bible was in the middle of the floor like he had been reading it. I knew from past experiences, when you're searching for answers and are really out there on drugs, the Bible is always what seems to come to mind when you are at your lowest point. That let me know someone, most likely his family, were believers and he knew about Jesus whether he was living for Him or not. He had been introduced to the Word at some point in his life.

Chris was locked in the truck and was too out of it to figure out how to unlock the doors. Craig had to go outside in the middle of the night and bust out the window so he could get out. Things always seem to get out of hand when meth is involved and that's just something that comes with it. Drama, chaos, and confusion — all these things are involved when you're living in the drug world.

They ended up leaving.

A few days later, after I had gone home and come down, I called up Chris and Charlie, looking to get high. They came to pick me up. The next I remember is a whole month had gone by. We were all rolling pretty tight. I came to the realization I had been high every single day for the past month. I hadn't ever stayed high that long. I would either run out of money or couldn't find anyone who was holding and was forced to come down. There were always dry periods when the dope man would run out, or someone in the circle got busted and I had to lay low. Then I would have to network and find a new hookup. The devil always opened a door for me to be able to find drugs. That was the trap that was always my downfall. I couldn't ever resist the temptation of getting high.

14

CHAPTER 14

My Dwelling Place: Darkness

By this point in my life I was getting high on a whole different level. Before it was just recreational. These people were running a business. They sold dope to survive. They were on the run from Owensboro, Kentucky for dealing and manufacturing meth. They were looking for connections out of state and they found some, me always getting in the middle of things so I could get high. I had hooked up with the wrong people. I needed them for rides, but clearly, I couldn't see past the fact that this made it easier for me to get high.

They needed me because I was familiar with this area and could easily find whatever it was that we needed. I knew people in my family that had everything needed to make meth. I began to introduce them to people that had known me for years. They trusted me so they trusted the people I was with. I introduced them to a way to make meth which was called "shake and bake."

That's what everyone was doing because anhydrous ammonia wasn't as easy to come by anymore. Farmers were selling it by the gallon making money off of it. I was able to get to it and I also knew people who specialized in cooking both.

Chris and Charlie looked at me as someone they could use to find every resource, and trustworthy enough to take advantage of. I thought we were all friends. They kind of felt like my family. I spent days, nights, and several months at a time with them. I really liked hanging out with them. I had no ulterior motives but to hang out, get high, and have a good time. I had no intentions of trying to get over on anyone. I always tried to treat everyone fairly.

I expected them to be the same way. I learned really quickly they were into a lot of things I wanted no part in.

Pretty soon they started ripping me off and cutting me out of things. I gave them all of their connections, locations out in the country where we would be safe, and they were ripping me off the whole time. I eventually caught on towards the end.

After several months of sleepless nights and staying up on meth too many days, I found myself in a realm where I could barely function. I had been up for so many days. Me and the "Juice Guy," who was one of our partners, got into it on my dad's farm about the way he was smoking it off. We ended up arguing over it. I was tripping, but as soon as we finished, we all got high and our problem was resolved. They didn't smoke it all off, just enough for us all to get high — about a gram each. In all reality, it should have been 4 or 5 grams a piece. That was the part that they were getting over on me, simply because I trusted them and didn't really know exactly how much it all was supposed to weigh. So, they kept more for themselves, but made it look like an even split when I was around. I just wasn't that kind of person.

That particular day we were on our way back from the barn in Princeton and going down Highway 41. We were all smoking, passing the pipe around. On our trip we decided to go to Owensboro. I don't remember anything except they said I was having a meth psychosis and was acting really weird. They said I was looking at them like I didn't know them and running back and forth to the door, freaked out.

They gave me a jar with a filter in it that had all the dope in the filter. That was the point, giving me a high dosage of methamphetamine to snap me out of whatever it was I was in. I had been up for 11 or 12 days straight and had eaten nothing. I was functioning off of meth, alcohol, and cigarettes. My body had to shut down. Charlie was on the bed sleeping and Chris and Juice were on their way to Walmart. They figured they would leave and I would eventually go to sleep. I remember thinking, since my sister was in Owensboro, she was going to pick me up. In my head I was getting ready for my ride and Ashley was on the way.

One of the reasons I was in Owensboro in the first place was because I needed Ashley and one of her friends to buy me a box of Sudafed. My sister, Ashley, was in rehab. How ridiculously insane is it to trade dope with people in rehab. That was just wrong, just another example of how my morals and values totally went down the drain. I was in way over my head with people who would take advantage of me and drop me like a bad habit.

I know it was the Holy Spirit who prompted me to walk down the hallway in a hotel to a room at the end of the hall. The door was cracked, so I went in and lay down on the floor right beside the bed. I remember thinking that if I lay on the floor behind the bed no one would see that I was in there.

I slept exactly two hours before I woke straight up out of a dead sleep and realized where I was and walked right back down the hall to the room I was previously in.

After some time, they came in and said they couldn't find me.

I told them where I had been, but they didn't believe me.

I said, "Come down the hallway. I will show you this room that is unlocked."

So, we walked right down the hall to the room I had just came from. I had purposely left the door cracked because that was exactly how I found it, but it was shut. I don't know what they thought I did or where I went but they didn't believe me. I even had the bag of dope in my bra that we all split supposedly four ways. It was only about a gram that they split with me. I'm sure they had a few grams apiece. They had sold theirs for money and I remember "Juice Man" asking he if he could have a little to put in his rig because he had already sold his. I was always generous and never told anyone no. I didn't want to see anyone go without because I knew, if I were in the same situation, I would want someone to share with me.

I had gone over the top this time. Shortly after that, I passed out on the end of the bed in a hotel room we were in. I was comatose and completely unconscious. I had been up a few more days. My body was locked. It was like I couldn't even comprehend enough to put my feet on the floor.

I remember Charlie saying in a stern manner, "Feet on the floor!" Then she repeated, "Feet on the floor!"

I was so out of it. I remember trying to do just that, but my body couldn't register what my mind was telling it to do. Finally, I was able to put my feet on the floor and stand up.

We were all being reckless, not eating, staying up for so many days. Charlie was like a mother hen to the four of us. She tried to keep us all in line to a certain extent, but it was like we were fearless, lawless, and rebellious. The world we were living in was all about drugs, selling, manufacturing, and just getting high and staying high. We were in our own little world — the meth world.

Shortly after that, I remember it was around Christmas time, we were all trying to get one last batch in. I was going home for Christmas. I knew I had to make it home by at least Christmas Eve. We had just gone back to the barn and made a batch. They didn't want to smoke it off there because then I would see how much we were pulling off of a batch. They wouldn't be able to rip me off around my family. They would have definitely called them out on it. They would rather just smoke half of it off and keep the rest to smoke off later to keep for themselves. We went to a hotel on Christmas Eve and I was just waiting to get my dope and go home. Charlie was planning on going to see her kids for Christmas. She hadn't seen them in a long time. She insisted that no one could touch it until she got back. I just wanted everyone to sit and wait in that hotel room until she got back to get what was rightly ours.

I was smoking like there was no tomorrow. I sat up in a corner trying to get my mind right so I could find the nerve to go home. I hadn't been home in forever. I was sitting in the corner looking pitiful, trying to get high off of dope. I had relentlessly been smoking for hours. I saw him holding up numbers above his head. I'm not sure how but I figured out exactly what it was that he was doing. We had made 24 grams of meth, but they would tell me we pulled 12 grams which would be split four ways. I went home for a holiday break with 3 grams of dope when I should have had 6 grams.

They had been cutting me out the whole time we were supposedly running a business. We were a team, which to me felt a lot like family. We spent every day together, lived in hotel rooms together, traveled all over the state of Indiana together manufacturing and selling drugs. The truth is there was no real loyalty with these people. They were all about themselves and the drugs. They would have gotten rid of me a lot sooner if they hadn't desperately needed me. Everything they needed they had to go through me to get. I had showed them a whole new way of self-destructing, how to create an endless amount of the drugs we were addicted to. My intentions were always to split everything fair and square. I was never the type of person to try and intentionally get over on people. I was in a very dark place overtaken by drugs and sucked in this self-destructive lifestyle that had me by the throat.

During this time I was in my mother's living room while she was at work and the Holy Spirit spoke through me and said, "You have to get sober. You can't continue on like this."

The enemy said quickly, "Why not? Who is going to stop you?"

I was in a spiritual battle within myself and that time my flesh won. I didn't have any spiritual weapons to fight with. I was so used to feeding my flesh and my Spirit was weak at this point, weaker than the mental obsession of addiction I was used to battling every day. I gave up fighting and just bowed down to it and accepted the fact this was who I was and was something I no longer had control over, completely powerless over.

After all of my years of addiction, this was a season of completely giving up and letting go of all hope of ever being sober. I had learned to accept the fact that I had made too many bad choices and been going down the wrong path for way too long to turn back now. The enemy had me convinced that darkness was my dwelling place. There was no longer any light or life inside me, which forced me to operate out of the flesh in a spirit of rebellion and desperation, which led to living in a realm where drugs and alcohol was all I needed to live. I didn't have any motivation to do anything. When I woke up, I was already figuring out a way I was going to get hold of the drugs I needed, whether it was meth or pills. A six-pack and a pack of cigarettes was something I had to have, if nothing else.

15

CHAPTER 15

Saved By Grace Again

I knew this ride wasn't going to last much longer. It always came to an end sooner or later. Chris and Charlie were already starting to distance themselves from me. They had replaced me with one of Chris' cousins who was also from Owensboro. They were making it, then handing it over to him since he was family and felt like they could trust him to sell, while they just stayed back and relaxed in the hotel room. They gave him their truck and in return he was making money for them. They quit answering my phone calls and never came back to pick me up. So now I was forced to get sober.

It had been about a week since I had seen them or had any dope. I had caught up on my rest and desperately needed to get high. I had been used to having it every day for almost a year straight and to go cold turkey was something I was not prepared to do. I was bound and determined to find a way to get to them because I knew they had dope. They never ran out. I had my sister and one of her friends take me to the hotel room that they were at. They needed a ride, so I offered to have my sister take them where they needed to go. In return, all I wanted to do was get high. I got there and we hung out for a while. They tried to tell me they were almost out, but that after they got back we would smoke a little bit. They left with my sister while me and my sister's friend waited in the hotel. After a while, I got a call saying Chris and Charlie were on their way to jail. My sister had run a red light and they got pulled over. They tried to run, but one of the police officers pulled the stun gun on Charlie because they were running. My sister told us to get out of the hotel room, that the police were on the way. So, I grabbed a few filters that were put back in the closet and stuck them down my pants and we left. Of course, I was always spared. They let my sister go and told her she didn't need to be hanging around these kind of people. They were on the run and had all kinds of drug paraphernalia on them and were wanted in Owensboro for the same exact thing. That was a blessing in disguise because I could have easily been caught up in all that, but the Lord knew the plans He had for me and I just thought I was lucky. My entire life the Lord had me hidden for Himself and never allowed me to get busted when everyone else around me always got caught. The Lord delivered me from the trap the enemy had set for me many times. That's one trap the Lord never let me fall into.

Charlie was released and Chris took all the charges. The first place she came to was my house. She was on the back of a Harley with some guy she had hitched a ride with walking down Highway 41 when she was released from the county jail. She said we had to go to Owensboro to find a way to re-up so we could bail Chris out of jail.

I knew it was over. Once everyone gets busted it's a wrap. She was focused on bailing Chris out of jail and she wanted me to come with her. I knew in my Spirit it was time to sever ties between us. I didn't want any part of what she was trying to get us involved in. They had left me high and dry and I knew where they stood as far as I was concerned. I didn't trust her. I knew it was just a matter of time and that Chris wouldn't be getting out. So, I gave her my phone, told her to leave, and I would catch up with her in the next couple days. I had to get rid of her. She was hot and I was finished. She took my phone and I waited until she got where she was going, then I had my mom turn off my phone. It was in my mom's name. I was smart enough to know that everything she was doing could fall back on me if I wasn't careful. I heard through the grapevine a couple of weeks later that they had been released only to be caught in the act again. Finally, they were caught in their hometown. They had been being watched for years. I was at home when it all happened.

Once again, saved by grace.

It was time for me to try and pick myself up and start all over — again. I seem to have been starting over my whole life.

Every time, I would manage to get to the point where I was barely functioning enough to start feeling good about myself. With what little bit of confidence I would build up within, I would somehow move forward.

The seeds of the Word had been planted inside of me as a child. I had the faith of a mustard seed. I would come to some realization that God would give me the strength to get back up, and He always did.

Erin was still in jail but about to get out within the next few months. I began to write her again. I told her how heartbroken I was, how my life had completely fallen apart, and that she was the only friend I had. I told her I was sorry for not writing her while me and Becca were together, but Becca was jealous of Erin to begin with and didn't want me writing her at all. She was controlling and I liked it. I was submissive and wanted to make her happy, so I quit writing Erin. She had a roommate who also dated women. She insisted

I write and that would help me get over my failed relationship. Erin knew me probably better than anyone and of course she knew if I had some other woman to replace the one I had I would be able to move on. I fell in love so easily. It was like we fell in love writing love letters to each other and this fake relationship gave me something to hold on to. The truth is, neither one of us knew the meaning of the word love. We were two broken people trying to build a relationship on top of the brokenness we were currently in and setting ourselves up for failure. So, we wrote each other and planned on being together when she got out of jail. What was I thinking? Was I so desperate as to just be with any woman who would give me some attention? What could possibly come out of two self-destructing individuals trying to fall in love on paper?

During my years of addiction, clearly the choices that I made were all influenced by drugs and alcohol. My way of thinking made absolutely no sense. My choices were never thought out. I always acted from emotions. I only did what felt good. Living a life of insanity and instant gratification was the only way I knew how to function. No wonder I had no direction in life. I was being guided by fleshly desires and was in the world.

The world I lived in was all about me and what I wanted and just having a good time. I never thought about the future, living day to day in an unseen prison full of darkness and there was no light.

Dawn was a new chapter in my love life. I hadn't the slightest idea of her background, her family, and who she really was as a person. I thought she was attractive, and she was interested in me, so why not? But I was reaching for something that I knew nothing about. Another trap the enemy had set for me and I fell in once again. I just wanted to love someone but those I chose to love had no intention of loving me back. You can't give what you don't have. We were both walking in darkness looking for light from somewhere or someone but never able to find what it was. We were so desperately needy. I know now, salvation, the peace of knowing whom you belong to — is Jesus Christ.

Erin got out of prison a few months before Dawn. Me and Erin got reacquainted and picked up right where we left off. Erin was trying to walk a straight line and was on drug court and probation. If she violated that by failing her breathalyzers or drug screens she would have to go back to prison. So now that we were both sober for the time being it was easy for us to still have that relationship we were used to having. I got a job at Donut Bank and was still living with my mom. I would ride the city bus to work in the mornings, start work at 5:30 a.m., and was usually off by noon, so me and Dawn would hang out and drink beer for the rest of the day. I would often stay with her at her best friend's house, the guy who picked her up from prison who allowed her to live in his house until she got herself together. This was something else I knew nothing about. Her best friend was in his early fifties and, apparently, they had been a lot closer than I had thought.

I was naive in a lot of ways and always gave a person the benefit of the doubt. I was in most ways an honest and loyal person when it came to relationships and expected the same in return, which was my first mistake. I had a lot of expectations that didn't exist in real life. I was always a hopeless romantic who lived in this fantasy world of happily-ever-after and together forever. Those were the standards I used to measure every relationship I was ever in. I had no idea of what a normal or even healthy relationship looked like.

Erin worked at the Donut Bank on the other side of town and actually helped me get this job. My supervisor's name was Shelly. She was gorgeous and of course I was more than attracted to her. She was your typical preppy white girl — blonde hair, blue eyes, always had her makeup just right. I loved going into work just so I could flirt with her. I never acted on it or crossed the line but if I had ever had the chance to be with her, I would have. She dated one of the owner's sons. He was wealthy, which was intimidating, and I knew she would never leave him, so I stayed in the safe zone. She was one of the most beautiful women I had ever seen in my life, and she liked me.

I would see her and her boyfriend at one of the strip clubs I went to every Saturday night and she saw how I was in action. We would talk openly about my relationship which made me believe Shelly was curious. She always told me I was too pretty for Dawn and I could do better. I was thinking, yeah, I sure would love to be with you. Our relationship was always slightly more than friendly and that's as far as it went.

This life was short-lived. Our time together was no different than any other relationship I had been in, the same destructive pattern. Eventually we ended up getting hold of some meth and, slowly but surely, everything I had worked toward, the life I had managed to rebuild, crumbled and eventually fell apart.

I hooked up with Craig and Britney, ended up getting too high, and couldn't show up for work the following day. The next thing you know, I was up for five days. I remember calling in every morning and telling my supervisor I had the flu. Erin got wind of that. I hadn't been answering her phone calls, so she decided to kindly repay me by snitching me out, letting the hiring manager of every Donut Bank in Evansville know that I was on one. The fact that I was hanging out with her sister Britney and she knew we were smoking dope was the icing on the cake. That's just how Erin was - jealous even to the extent of, instead of having my back, causing me to lose my job. She didn't see it that way. She felt betrayed because her sister and I were now drug buddies and I was spending time with her and not Erin.

CHAPTER 16

My Dirty Thirties

It was 2010 and I was now in my early thirties and had absolutely nothing to show for the years that had gone by. I was still struggling with drugs and alcohol, a never-ending battle I had been losing. A lifetime of happiness, I felt, was lost.

My mother had completely turned her life around. The struggle she had always faced seemed to have ceased. She was a woman of God who was now living a righteous life. She had made it through her trials and tribulations and had overcome financially. She had been at University of Evansville for well over 10 years and was able to provide and take care of all of us girls as we lived in her house in active addiction. She had been praying for us for years.

We would go to the church we had belonged to since we were kids. I went to church just to appease Mom. I knew it was important to her that we went. She was allowing us to live with her. The only one of us who worked most of the time was Erica. Mom made it known that if we were going to stay with her then we were required to go to church. She had seen all the hell I had been through and she was there through it all. Deep down I wanted to change and she knew it. There was a part of me that wanted desperately to find whatever it was that she had. I knew that Mom had this peace and this light that I couldn't quite put my finger on.

Her relationship with God was real. I had seen the change in her and I wanted to be like my mother. I felt like if she could make it then so could I. She had always raised us the right way. We grew up in the church, we were a praying family, and we were a team. The struggles she faced from being a single mother with four girls and no help was the direct result of the strength and the faith that she stood on and taught us to stand on. This Jesus I only knew from the Word of God, hearing it in the little Methodist Church on Lyles Station Road where I grew up.

The Word clearly declares in Proverbs 22:6 (NKJV) *"Train up a child in the way he should go, And when he is old he will not depart from it."*

My mother firmly believed in that. Thirty-five years later I saw the truth of that scripture manifest. I am living and walking testimony of that scripture.

Isaiah 55:11 (KJV) also says, *"So shall my word be that goeth forth out from my mouth: it shall not return unto me void, but it shall accomplish that which I please, and it shall accomplish that for which I please, and it shall prosper in the thing whereto I sent it."*

No matter what struggles I have faced or will face, all the darkness I have walked through, God's plan and purpose He has had for me before the foundations of the earth were formed will come forth and will be fulfilled, because He spoke it.

God has promised in His Word, "Everyone who calls on the name of the Lord will be saved."

I have called on his name and I know, "He is not a man that He shall lie."

Every promise He has spoken to me by his Spirit I believe with all my heart will come to pass. I am able to believe in myself only because I believe in Him. His Holy Spirit is what guides me and He has told me, "I will not let you fail," so I know everything I touch will prosper. I have not failed in anything I set out to do that He asked me to do and know I never will.

I had just got off a binge with Ashley and Lamar. I had been working at CRF, but I just quit one day. I had gotten way too high and fallen back into that lifestyle after being off of meth for about four or five months.

This was another relapse. I had quit for good and everyone I knew and been associated with pertaining to meth was in jail. I had started fresh, trying desperately to get back up, just to fall right back down.

I wasn't working a program, but I had started going back to church and hanging out with my mom. She was always there to help me try and get myself together. She was my only true friend and loved me unconditionally through it all. She knew the hold addiction had always had on me, and the trials and tribulations my entire family faced against alcoholism on both my mother and father's sides. I was still drinking, taking pills every once in a while, but I was trying to let go as best I could. I had been in active addiction my entire life. I didn't know how to live any other way. I couldn't really even function without alcohol when drugs were no longer a part of my life. This mental obsession would win every time. I didn't know how to quit.

Me, Erica, Bre, and my niece, Ellie, all lived together with Mom on Burdette Street. This was the last chapter of us living together as a family. I remember lying in my bed for days from depression and trying to find something to live for. I remember this beautiful woman named Amber who I was infatuated with. I was in the process of trying to get to know her before I relapsed. She was drop-dead gorgeous. I felt this connection with her, that I later found to be spiritual, but my flesh wanted to be with her. I felt that she was definitely out of my league but that wasn't reason enough to stop me. As I was lying in bed, if I found a reason for not giving up it was her.

I sobered up and walked to CRF and talked to Mark, who I had known for years. I worked at CRF in the beginning at the age of 20, and over the years they had shown me mercy and were always willing to give me another chance. I was going to be honest with Mark about relapsing and trying to get my life together and for that I asked him to show me mercy one last time, and he did. I was blessed. I thanked the Lord for giving me the only job I felt like I was good at. I had spent the last 10 years working off and on for CRF, so it felt like home.

I picked up right where I left off with Amber. She was my motivation. She gave me a reason to keep going. I barely even knew her. We flirted in random conversations but I was drawn by her. I don't know what it was, I just had to have her, and I wasn't stopping until she went out with me.

Her birthday was coming up and she made it very clear that she was going out with her mom and that was it. She left no room for me to imply that I wanted to take her out. So, I decided to get her a birthday present and leave it on her desk to surprise her. I put a fifth of Grey Goose in a gift bag with a card. I couldn't wait for her to come in that morning. I was cheesing from ear to ear. I knew my smile was going to give it away, but I didn't care. I was happy to see her beautiful smile and the surprise on her face was priceless. That was it. That was the moment she allowed me in. That was the beginning of what was to come. I was already in love with her and now all I wanted was the chance to prove it to her.

One Friday night, her and a couple of girls that worked with us went to TGI Fridays to have some drinks. I remember talking to Emily on the phone. She was a friend of a friend and we also knew each other from work. She asked me to come and meet them for drinks. I didn't have a dollar in my pocket but my baby sister, Bre, happened to be a server in the bar, so I was going to ask her to cover me. I really didn't think it through. I thought she could cover me for at least one beer and I would figure it out. All I needed was to get out of the house.

We all decided to go Emily's house and drink some more. Amber wasn't drinking that night, but me and Emily were getting hammered. I remember just talking to Emily most of the night. We were both buzzed and, since I had her to talk to, I wasn't so nervous around Amber. I remember she wasn't feeling so well that night. She was cramping and asked me to rub her back for her.

I was like, "Of course I will."

That was a point of contact that allowed her and I to gradually cross the line and become more than friends. I was falling more and more in love with her every day. It was the way that she carried herself, which was different than most of the other women I had been with. She walked in confidence. She was beautiful but not vain. She would dress feminine, but she had a little hood in her, which was what attracted me to her the most. I was never attracted to anyone like her. My type had always been preppy white girls, but this girl could rock some J's, a wife beater and some sweats, and have me completely mesmerized. You talk about fine — and she also seemed to be highly intelligent. I couldn't see how someone like her was working at a job like CRF with me. She looked like someone who would be in a professional field of some kind, nursing or banking.

Just like everyone else, she was in a dark place at one time and found herself lost and bound in addiction. She had a great heart and was always encouraging me. She had a good job before and dabbled in the wrong thing and lost the opportunities she had been given and had to start over. Her testimony actually inspired me. I saw how anyone could get caught up in addiction but that there was a way out. She still struggled with a couple of things, but her faith in God and the spiritual connection she had with Him drew me to her even more.

She had been introduced to the things of the Spirit long before I even thought about walking in the Spirit. The stories she told me of the miracles, signs, and wonders she had witnessed firsthand I believed with all my heart. We were connected Spiritually, and I knew what she was sharing was truth. I knew what it was like to be so far away from God you can't even see a way back to Him. The darkness had blinded us both and we were both trying to find our way back, but the enemy came in and twisted and camouflaged what was meant for good into something evil.

What I thought was love was really lust. The pureness I once knew I saw in her. The hope and encouragement she gave me led me to trust her. The feelings and emotions I had toward her were mistaken to be of God, when in all reality it was the enemy. I believed the lie. The time and conversations we had with each other were real and there was nothing fake about her. I was inspired to the point that I felt she would be a good influence on me. I tried to let go of the hard drugs and just drink my beer every day, desperately trying to get myself together and pick up the pieces of everything that was lost and broken. I was calling out to the Lord and honestly seeking Him, but my flesh would not let go of the bondages of homosexuality and addiction. The enemy was actually using me to cause her to stumble. The enemy was using me to pull her in to this darkness I was so deep into. I couldn't see the truth. All I wanted to do was love her. I wanted nothing but the best for her. Now looking back, I was causing her to sin.

We spent every hour of every day together. I was happy with her. She had a job, a car, a home, and a license — things I had lost along the way — so I looked up to her. I thought she must be doing something right.

She was responsible in areas I was not and strong in ways that I was weak. I was loving and caring and sensitive to her feelings and she clearly saw the good in me.

I had a cousin I hung out with all the time who she was mutual friends with. My cousin had nothing but good things to say about me, so Amber trusted me. We were in love. I think I fell a little harder than she did. She sometimes drew this line with me and would put up this wall because she had been hurt before, then immediately realize it was me and I had no intentions of hurting her. I was always loyal. She had my head spinning. I was so whipped I couldn't even think about looking in any other direction. I think that's what scared her about me. I'm definitely one of a kind and, back then, extremely co-dependent. She in fact was very independent, something I had always wanted to be.

Valentine's Day was coming up and, since we were in a relationship, I wanted to get her something, but she told me not to. I assumed it was because she kind of wanted to keep our relationship secret, which most women do. I wanted to respect her feelings and didn't want to push the issue. Big mistake! I knew I should have gone ahead and got her something. That was on my heart, but I didn't want to ruin things.

She had quit smoking and was having a hard time with that. I was a smoker, so that certainly didn't make things any easier. I tried not to smoke around her and would sometimes go outside to smoke. She said as long as she could smell it once in a while, she was okay. The truth is Amber was feeling conviction for being in a relationship with me. I didn't figure it out until several years later. She was pulling away from me in an indirect way.

She called me crying in the middle of her living room one night and said she didn't know what was wrong. I told her to call on Jesus and He would give her an answer. He did. She was feeling the conviction of the Holy Spirit. We never talked about what the Lord spoke to her, but I had a pretty good feeling in my Spirit what was going on. Shortly after that things began falling apart.

I wasn't feeling any conviction. My heart had been hardened for so long, I believed the lie. But believe me, God had an understanding. I always told anyone who asked me where I stand with God, being gay.

I said, "When I stand before him on judgement day, I will tell him it's always been in my heart." I truly believed that the Lord would understand and allow me to go home with Him when He comes for us. I could have never been more wrong.

The Bible declares in 1 Corinthians 6:9-10 (NKJV), *"Do you not know that the unrighteous will not inherit the kingdom of God? Do not be deceived. Neither fornicators, nor idolaters, nor adulterers, nor homosexuals, nor sodomites, nor thieves, nor covetous, nor drunkards, nor revilers, nor extortioners will inherit the kingdom of God. And such were some of you."*

(I was one of these people.)

"But you were washed, but you were sanctified, but you were justified in the name of the Lord Jesus and by the Spirit of our God." (1 Corinthians 6:11, NKJV)

Amber took heed to the Holy Spirit and ended our relationship. She told me that we were too serious and she just wanted to be friends. That literally broke my heart into a thousand pieces. I adored her. After you cross that line things can never be the same. I had lost my best friend and my lover. We tried to just be cool, but the enemy came and does what he does best and just leave a huge mess. I felt rejected and couldn't deal with the heartbreak and the pain I was experiencing.

I had gotten myself together to a certain extent. I was happy with myself, I was working, and found just enough hope to keep moving forward. Then the unthinkable happened. She started talking to this guy who had been trying to get with her the whole time we were dating. He worked with us and now was his chance to swoop in, and he did. I was at work one day and I used her phone. I always used her cell because I didn't have one at the time. I was calling my cousin, Christa, because I couldn't take it anymore, working with Amber every day. It was weird. I couldn't concentrate. She was flirting with this guy and I didn't like it.

I remember something welling up inside of me and I felt like I was going to break down and start crying right there at work. So, while I had her phone, I saw text messages where they had been texting back and forth.

That was it for me. I had to get out of there. I felt heartbroken and on the verge of an emotional breakdown. I left immediately and my cousin pulled up.

I said, "I gotta go get high. Amber is talking to someone else. I am having a bad day."

How could she do this to me? It didn't take her long to move on. Did she even have any feelings for me at all? Was all this just my imagination? Was I the only one who had been in love? I knew she had feelings for me. She did what she felt like was right, but I was left devastated. My heart felt like it was literally ripped out of my chest.

I went with my cousin to the Dope Girl's house. It was a wrap. I was on a good one.

I quit my job. I didn't dare walk through those doors and feel the way I felt that day.

For a few weeks, all I did was talk about Amber and how much I missed her. I'm sure everyone got tired of hearing it, especially Donna.

She told my cousin, Christa, "If I hear one more thing about that girl I'm going to throw up."

I ended up hanging out with her almost every day. She started having feelings towards me and I was vulnerable, heartbroken, and really needed a friend. She was there and I had fallen into a deep depression. My addiction jumped right back in. With her, I had an unlimited supply. So, I got back into business, if that's what you call it.

I was spiraling out of control and didn't know how to stop. I stayed with Donna and her mother in a dope house with no electricity.

I wasn't sure of what step to take next. I didn't have a job and I never went home to my mom's, spun out on drugs like I was. I had quit my job and couldn't face her again. It wasn't that long ago that I was in this same situation and here I was again at the bottom of the barrel, on another road full of destruction. And it gets worse every single time you go back out. I needed to take control of my life and seek God. That I was unable to do. I used the only thing I knew to ease the pain and deal with what my life consisted of, which was absolutely nothing. I fell and I fell hard. The way I was choosing to live was ridiculous. It had been a long time since I had fallen this low. I was living life like a savage, just waiting to get my next fix, doing whatever I had to get it. It was my life.

Donna and I were like Bonnie and Clyde. To be honest, out of all the women I had been with, I trusted her the most. I knew she would never leave me. I was a prize to her. To her I was beautiful. I had respect for others and I tried to lead her in the right direction. I had a good heart and she saw that. She fell for me like I fell for Amber. The fact that she loved me the best she could was enough for me. She put no expectations on me, and I had none for her. I did expect her to have some morals, values, and common sense. She was reckless and I knew it. I tried to put a steering wheel on her because I knew, if I didn't, we would both be in jail.

I remember I had a feeling — the one I always had when something was about to go down. I felt it in my Spirit. I begged her, "Look, we need to slow down. Things are getting out of hand. Too much is going on. Let's get away for a while, just me and you. We have to get away from everyone and rethink the situation we are currently in." We were both staying up way too long. She was more reckless than I had ever seen her. I couldn't shut her down.

That coming weekend, we were going camping. She was getting everything together that we were going to need. She was getting a batch ready and we were at the house of my old drug buddy. She had just finished and we all got high, but I was higher than I had been in a long time. She was so spun out. Her mom and I dropped her off so she could get rid of it.

Me and my buddy went to Walmart to get camping supplies. I knew something was up because her mom called me and said the police had come to her house looking for her. We went back to my buddy's house where we originally were. I was going to find her. As soon as we were parked, the Feds had guns in our faces and said, "Freeze. You're under arrest."

I was dumbfounded. Me and my buddy were both higher than a kite. I had absolutely nothing on me. My buddy didn't say a word. The Feds had gotten a call that

Donna was manufacturing meth and had raided his house. Someone had told on her and led the Feds right to the location. My buddy got busted because it was in his house and they were looking for Donna. They were going to let me go.

I couldn't sit still. I was extremely nervous. I overheard one of the police officers say, "We're letting her go? Look at her. She can't sit still."

So, he came over and asked me what I went to Walmart for, and I told him I was going camping.

Then he asked, "With who?"

I said, "My girl."

He said, "Who is your girl?"

I said, "Donna."

Then I heard him say, "You're going to jail!"

So, I went to jail for the night.

They didn't put any charges on me because, once again, the grace of God was on me. Even through my addiction and my disobedience I always had the hand of God over my life, even in my darkest times. This was a very dark time for me. I was in the holding cell before Donna. Then I heard her voice. She came in and said, "I should have listened to you."

I told her, "We should have gone away and none of this would have happened."

The truth is this was God's will. He was putting all this to a halt. Once again, I was set free but still in bondage. She told me, "I'm going to be in here for a long time." That was it. We said our goodbyes. I called Mom to pick me up from jail the following day. Mom and Dan came to pick me up and take me home. She stopped and bought me a pack of cigarettes and told me there was some fried chicken and sides for me to eat and to get some rest. So, I did just that.

Here I was again, all alone with nothing but a broken heart and a lot of bad habits. I was so lost. Everyone around me was getting busted, getting locked up left and right. I turned off my phone and stayed at Mom's house, trying to get sober again, going back to my six-pack of beer every night. I was sick and tired of being sick and tired.

At this time Mom had given us six months to get our own place. Her and Dan were eventually going to get married and she was going to move in with him in Newburgh. Mom deserved it. She was paying all the bills and we were going nowhere in life. She was ready to start a new chapter and move on. She had been supporting us all for way too long — our entire lives. She just wanted us to get better and, clearly, we were not. Time was ticking and we were all doing the same old thing — not working and not looking for a place, thinking we still had forever. But time was almost up.

Mom told us we could keep everything in the house. She gave us our beds and distributed out the furniture evenly. I had nowhere to go but back to the dope house. I moved in with Donna's mom, expecting her to be a mom and take care of me. She was living a life of addiction and had been for over 30 years. She was going to show me how to survive living off the streets. This is all I had, so I tried to make the best of it. I had always used Mom's house to shower, eat, and do laundry. I had been able to always have good hygiene. But my whole lifestyle was about to change. I was slumming it.

I was selling cable instead of a kid's charity. It was within walking distance of where Linda lived, and I figured I could walk to work every day. It was so hard to try to even function. I had to go different places to take a shower and my clothes no longer smelled fresh like Downy. In fact, I was looking really dingy.

I came in contact with a friend of mine that also worked at TeleDirect. We had known each other by drug association. She had just gotten out of prison, trying to get herself together.

She took one look at me and said, "Wow, you're skinny!" That time I knew it wasn't a compliment. She used to always say how beautiful I was and how well I dressed and now she looked at me like, "What in the world happened to you?"

I told her I was staying down the street with Linda and she said, "I can tell. You are starting to dress like her."

That wasn't a compliment either, but it was the truth. I would later run into this young lady but the circumstances, by the grace of God, were totally different.

After my first couple of paychecks I did what I've always done. As soon as I got my paycheck, I was on one. I went straight to the dope man and smoked up my entire paycheck. What a pitiful shame. Linda was okay with it, but as soon as I quit my job, she sent me packing. I could no longer supply both of our habits and I didn't share my last with her. I shared it with someone else. She went on a ranting-and-raving episode. She called my sister and asked me to leave. I needed to get out of there anyway. I needed to go and get help.

After about a week at my sister's, eating, sleeping, and being sober, I went back out ready to get on another one. I ended up hooking up with this girl who I had known a couple of years back and we were getting high. She stayed with this guy named Noah on Grand Street in the hood. I was helplessly walking the streets, nowhere to sleep, no money, and just trying to find my next fix. I was empty-handed, crying out in my despair. I remember one day I hit my knees on the concrete and all I could scream was, "God help!"

I walked back to Noah's on Grand Street to Brandi, another woman I was trying to hook up with. Really, I just needed a place to stay. She was homeless, too. We were all in the same shape, struggling every single day, living in a dope house. Something was bound to happen.

This guy Chuck, who was Noah's cousin, came in from time to time. This guy was bad news. He was on a whole other level of evil. We were all hanging out one day at Noah's and I called Blake, who was one of my best friends at the time. He had dated my sister, Erica. He came over with this random girl. They had a few grams of dope and some pills and came over to share with me and make some money. Secretly, Chuck was planning to rob him. I was sitting on the couch and suddenly I heard a loud clank. It was the sound of the lock on the front door. Chuck and this guy who was in the back room had a gun and a knife ready. They made us all go in the kitchen in the back. They made everybody drop their pants and took the dope and pills from them. I was shocked. I had no idea this was going down. But I was there so it made me a part of it. I didn't get robbed because I didn't have anything. They made us all get high and then they told them to leave. I didn't leave because I was staying there.

When they left, Chuck and O' boy split the money and drugs. We got high and they left. Blake went back and told my sisters I robbed them because I was a part of it. I was just as much a victim as they were; I just didn't have anything to take. So now my family was against me. Things just kept getting worse. No one wanted to be around me. I felt like there was no way out. A few more weeks of deep depression and even more drug use.

I had been up for about five days. Chuck said he was about to come make a batch and to be ready. I knew that meant more dope, so I was more than ready. We did what we had to do. I was the clean-up person.

A few hours later Blake came by. It was just us three in the room. Noah was in his bedroom where he always stayed due to a heart condition he was battling. I was cleaning up and Blake and Chuck were in a bedroom closest to the porch so they could see everything out of the window into the street. This front window was broken and needed repairing but no one was going to spend money on repairing a broken window.

We were all homeless. Any money we had went toward drugs and alcohol.

Then the completely unexpected happened. Chuck couldn't find his glock. I knew he'd had it. I had been with him all day. I was scared to be around guns and drugs. I knew those two never mix and I didn't want any part of handling a gun. All of a sudden, I saw Chuck grab this baseball bat and was getting ready to start swinging. Me and Blake immediately stood up in shock, wondering what in the world was going on. We were standing directly in front of the window and he said, "Pull your pants down and put your hands up!"

So we did. I was so scared and in shock. I was lost for words. I was about to get beaten with a baseball bat for no reason at all. This situation went from casually hanging out to a burglary. Someone was about to get hurt real bad or even killed.

Then Blake called Chuck in the other room and said, "Where all she been?" insinuating I was the one who stole it and possibly hid it.

He knew exactly where it was and acted as if he was looking for it and found it. The next thing I knew, they both walked back in the bedroom and I got punched on my forehead, right above my eye.

Chuck had pulled a punch on me. Somehow, I didn't lose my balance. I was completely off guard and standing directly in front of a broken window. Clearly, I should have fallen backwards, and I would have surely died from broken shards of glass piercing and stabbing through my body, falling through that broken window. With the combination of extremely sharp edges and acceleration from gravity, there was barely a chance for survival.

Nothing but the hand of God Himself and His warring angels coming from the heavens saved me. Even while I was drowning in sin in the midst of darkness, He spared me. I didn't fall through that window, but my head busted open.

I realized I had been sucker punched by a grown man and accused of a crime I did not commit. I was pleading and crying, telling them I didn't do it. All the while I had lost control of my bladder in front of everyone.

Then my sister Erica walked in. She didn't say one word. She sat down in shock, wondering what had just happened. Chuck saw that. Erica's response let him think that Erica must have thought I did something shady, that it wasn't out of character for me to steal.

Erica took me in the other room still completely silent, cleaned up my forehead, and gave me a pair of clean jeans I had lying around in the living room where I slept. We went back into the room and acted like nothing even happened.

Chuck said, "I'm still going to give you some dope and we are going to finish what we started."

He apologized to Noah, telling him how he had been up for a couple of days and lost his head. Noah gave me a hug as Chuck briefly left the room. He was consoling me the best he could. We had become good friends. After all, he was allowing me to live in his house.

Chuck came back into the room. We were all three sitting in a circle, waiting for our batch to get finished so we could split it between us and go our separate ways. Erica was leaving, so Blake walked her out to the truck to talk a while.

Noah kept telling Chuck, "Man, I don't think she did it."

Realizing Blake was the one who led Chuck to the gun, he realized he may have framed me.

A little later when Blake came back in the room, Chuck said to me, "If you didn't do it, then he did. If you are innocent, I'm a give you my gun. Shoot him in the foot."

He was serious.

I said, "No! I can't do that."

He said, "Well, you're the one who took the blame then." From past experience, I knew this was not the time to be firing gunshots, not with a meth lab in the house.

I waited until it was done and went in the basement with Blake to get high. We did a shot and he kept telling me that all this happened because Chuck had been up for too many days and hid the gun or lost it himself. I didn't care at this time. What's done is done. I knew Blake did it, but I couldn't prove it.

I took off walking with about a gram of dope. I wasn't even high. I guess all that trauma and chaos had me so shook up I couldn't even get high. I walked over to a guy I knew. His apartment building was right off of Highway 41. It was about a mile and a half away. It was around 9 or 10 p.m. I had no business walking around town with a busted forehead and a bruised eye, just leaving a meth lab. I was so shaken. I remember I dropped a bag on the way there. What a mess!

This was my life, the road I was on, and the only way I knew. I was lost!

How do you get so lost?

It seemed as if this was the end of the road for me. It couldn't get any darker than this. I felt it would be better if I just got hit by one of those semis going down Highway 41. I was listening to the wrong voice. I ended up at my sister's. I was couch surfing, staying from place to place. I was tired, fatigued, and sleep deprived. I hardly had anything in me. I felt like I was going to literally fall over and die.

I managed to stumble into Linda's, the house with no electricity. She said I looked really bad. She told me to go lie in her bed. I slept for three days straight. She brought me food and water three times a day. Linda knew how to survive on the streets. She had been living that way for over 30 years. I managed to get enough strength to get up and go take a shower over at her daughter, Aimee's, house. Aimee and I knew each other very well. I used to date her sister and we always looked out for each other. She was my guardian angel. This apartment had electricity and I could shower and do laundry. I jumped in the shower and laid on the couch for three more days. I was in bad shape. I was near death and didn't even know it.

The devil was trying to kill me. He had attempted to take my life many times and every time the hand of God would protect me and I would not die. Just like a couple years back when I was cooking dope and my face caught fire. Still until this day Samantha says she remembers seeing my entire face catch fire, then it disappeared, just like the story in the Bible of Shadrach, Meshach, and Abednego. They were the three Hebrew men in Daniel 3 who were thrown into a fiery furnace by Nebuchadnezzar, king of Babylon, when they refused to bow down to the King's image. The three were preserved from harm and the king saw four men walking in the flames — the fourth, like the son of God, delivered them from death by fire, just as He delivered me from death by fire that day. I will never forget.

Aimee took care of me the best she could. She washed my clothes for me and nursed me back to health. I was in a safe haven and she made sure I had three meals a day. She brought them to me and when I was finished, she did my dishes. I will never forget that act of kindness. Jesus used her to save my life. I had a peace for the first time in a long time and I knew I could finally rest. I would have been found dead somewhere if it wasn't for my Protector and Savior, Lord Jesus. I didn't even know Him, but He knew me.

He says in the scriptures, "Before I formed you in the womb I knew you, before you were born I set you apart and appointed you as my prophet to the nations."

I know this to be true. I was always known by God. He has always loved me even when I didn't deserve it. I have been forgiven much.

Luke 7:47 (NIV) says, *"Therefore, I tell you, her many sins have been forgiven — as her great love has shown. But whoever has been forgiven little, loves little."*

I ended up leaving with my cousin after I was nursed back to health and we went back to that same house I was in before to get a bag of dope. I wasn't scared. That was old news. I bought a bag from him and he, in his own way, told me that was his bad and he had been up for too long, that Blake had admitted to one of his friends that he was the one who stole the gun and I took the hit.

I said, "I told you I didn't do it."

We had too much going on. I'm the one who really kept a clear head enough to prevent us all from getting manufacturing charges. We were cool after that. He hooked me up for free every time he saw me.

I still ran the streets. I ended up back at my sister Ashley's. This time it was different. My younger sisters were still all there together and when I came it rocked the boat. She ended up asking us all to leave and I knew I had to make a change.

I suddenly remembered what my bunkie had said when I was in jail for 23 days. She told me about this rehab in Louisville called Wayside. I felt the tugging of the Holy Spirit. I had been sober for a couple of weeks, long enough to clearly think through a plan. I was done.

I knew I didn't have an ID. I'd lost it and had nothing. I needed to get one. I didn't keep up with my birth certificate or social security card. I couldn't even keep up with my ID. I hit my knees for the first time in a long time and I prayed to God. I made the phone call and they scheduled me to come on a Monday. It was Friday. They told me I had to have my ID, but I was just going to roll with it and see what happened. Maybe they would let me in anyhow.

The next morning my mother came over to give me gas money for Ashley to drive me to Louisville. She said she checked her P.O. Box and miraculously there was an envelope from the BMV that had my state ID in it. I hadn't even been to the license branch and my mom sure didn't know anything about it. It was a miracle. I knew the Lord had a hand in this and this is where He was sending me.

17

CHAPTER 17

Overcomer

Ashley and I hit the highway in 2012. Ashley was on fire for Jesus and was attending a full gospel church that operated in the gifts and five-fold ministry. All of us sisters went a time or two. They spoke in tongues and were filled with the Spirit. I thought it was weird, but it seemed to work for Ashley. We would clown Ashley and make fun of her for speaking in tongues and found it to be hilarious. Ashley didn't seem to mind. That's what sisters do. So, on the way to Louisville we worshipped the whole way and I was excited about what was to come. Anything was better than the life I was living.

I remember this particular song came on, "Overcomer" by Mandisa. Ashley knew that song and she dedicated that song to me. She spoke over me that this was my destiny; I was an overcomer — and I was.

We got to the hotel and I checked in. I had a room on the fifth floor. That was the recovery floor. The upper levels were rented out to the public.

They told me to get settled in, so I unpacked my trash bag. I tried to take everything in. I was very anxious and nervous.

Louisville was predominantly black and there were women from all over the United States. I felt like I was on vacation. I had my own bed and half of a room in a hotel that was ginormous to me. I hadn't been in a place so nice in such a long time. I was coming off the streets into what felt like a vacation resort. I was truly blessed to be in the place I was in and have the opportunity to get better — free of charge.

I had to sit in the lobby all day until 5 p.m., which was dinner time. They provided three meals a day and always had doughnuts and cakes in the cafeteria for us to eat at any time. I was content and spent most of my time reading the Big Book which they provided for us (it was for Alcoholics Anonymous) and writing my girlfriend, Rickelle, who was incarcerated at the time.

I had spent about 21 days in jail and while I was in there, Rickelle and I had gotten reacquainted while we were in there together.

My bunkie had told me about this rehab and I told her I had made up my mind I was going. Well here I was. I wrote to her daily to keep my mind occupied and to keep me from feeling lonely. I asked her to send me some money because I was completely broke and needed cigarettes. My mother had given me just enough for gas to get here. I knew Rickell's baby's daddy sent her money every week and had an endless supply and wouldn't mind helping me out if that's what she wanted. She sent me $50 and I was thankful.

About this time something changed inside of me. I started going to Miracle Life Church on Wednesday nights and I felt the Spirit of the Living God like I had never felt before. This church was a lot like Freedom, the tongue-talking church my sisters had been going to. They were on fire. Now I felt that fire! The first couple times I went I felt at home like I was supposed to be there. I loved the way Apostle Collins preached the Word and the full expression of worship I was experiencing. This was a little familiar to me and I was able to receive because I felt like I had found what my sisters had found back home, the power of the Holy Spirit. I knew it was real. I was able to hear, feel, and see the truth like I had never heard, felt, or seen anything in my entire life. I found God and I didn't want to let go. I was happy and so full of joy! I was blind and now I could see. I felt like a kid again, a kid who looked at the world with excitement and wonder. I had stepped into the light. I attended church on Wednesday nights and Sunday mornings and was reading my Bible every day. I was praying to the Lord at night listening to gospel music. I felt free for the first time in my life. I was on fire for Jesus.

I called my family with excitement, telling them how I found Jesus and was talking about the things of God. My mother was happy I was sober and knew I was safe but told me to be careful and only follow what the Bible said. She hadn't been introduced to speaking in tongues, but she was a woman of God and knew the Lord very well. Ashley, on the other hand, was already with the program. She knew exactly what I was experiencing. We were both on fire for Jesus and diligently seeking Him.

My way of thinking had already started to transform. It had only been a few weeks. All the cussing I did just went away. My sinful nature began to fade. This new creature was rising up inside of me. I was being transformed by the power and the Word of God.

They gave me a housekeeping job at Wayside. It was part of the program. They had different positions — the warehouse where they kept donations and gave them to us residents, the men's shelter close by, the hotel laundry, housekeeping, working in the café, and front desk — these were the jobs they offered the women in recovery and we worked almost full time. Instead of paying us wages, they gave us what they called a gift at the end of the week so we would have extra money for anything else we may need, cigarettes, snacks, hygiene. They also gave us the option of saving some of our money in safe-keeping so when we got out, we would have something to get us started. Life was great.

Then I got a letter from my girlfriend. My feelings had changed. I was feeling conviction. I just felt holding on to her was wrong. I hadn't felt conviction in a long time. My heart had been hard, but now my heart was open to receive the truth. The Word had taken root in my spirit.

I was filled up with living water, the kind that the Word tells about in John 4:14 (NIV): *"But whoever drinks the water I give them will never thirst. Indeed, the water I give them will become in them a spring of water welling up to eternal life."*

I had been touched by God. I would never be the same.

I decided not to write her anymore and to let go of anything and everything in my past linked to addiction and sin. I loved her but I just wanted a new beginning, a fresh start. This was my opportunity to let go. I couldn't manage to find the nerve to tell her on paper. I wanted out of this relationship. I didn't want to hurt her feelings and I didn't want her to think I just used her to get $50 dollars out of her and then forget all about her. So, I just held on to her letters. I still read them because I was lonely and I just wanted to feel some kind of affection, even if it was through the mail.

I continued to honestly work the program. I loved doing housekeeping. It was healing and also made me feel like I was being productive and contributing to society, functioning like a human being. I realized I didn't even know how to function. I had to be taught everything all over again, like a child.

We received $60 a week as our gift for the jobs we worked. I hadn't earned that much money in a long time. I actually started feeling good about myself. I was learning how to have a good work ethic. I woke up early in the mornings and went to morning meditation followed by our recovery classes until lunch. After lunch we went to work until dinner, then we went to our A.A. meetings or a church service outside of the hotel. That was mandatory, which helped us change our way of thinking.

My mom was proud of me. I called her a few times a week and she always encouraged me and sent me $40 every other week since she knew I was sober and was doing well. I was still receiving Rickelle's letters and reading them.

Then the Lord came to me in a dream.

In the dream I saw a staircase from heaven appear from the sky. It came directly in front of me and it was the image of Jesus. I was on my knees and I looked up and he shook his head saying, "No."

There were no words spoken. It was in my spirit, yet I understood and knew exactly what we were talking about.

Then I said to him, "But it's always been in my heart."

I was referring to the gay lifestyle I had been living all these years. Then He turned and went right back up the staircase to heaven.

I had never seen anything so beautiful and vivid in all my life. Not even in movies had I seen anything close to this realm of my dream. The Lord had come down to warn me Himself that my lifestyle was not okay. He simply shook his head no. I knew He forbid it and what the scriptures say is true. No one can ever tell me any different or convince me of anything else. I had heard from the Lord himself. I never had dreams from the Lord, ever. That was the first visitation from the Lord I received.

Apostle Collins said that everyone under his congregation had a visitation from the Lord. When I told him about the dream, he said that was a warning: "The Lord is beginning to show you heavenly things."

I loved Apostle Collins. He was part of the five-fold ministry. He operated in the gifts of healing and was under the mantle of an Apostle and Prophet. I was being introduced to the things of the Spirit and had received an impartation from God through Apostle Collins that I would carry with me through eternity. I loved going to his worship services. I was seeking the Lord with my whole heart and I wanted to be delivered.

I remember he preached on fasting and praying and I wondered if the Lord wanted me to fast.

The Bible's declaration in Matthew 17:21 (NASB) is a very powerful one: *"But this kind does not go out except by prayer and fasting."*

Everyone knows the power of prayer and its irremovable presence in the Spiritual life, but fasting and praying move things around in the Spiritual realm leading to deliverance. I wanted this deliverance but wasn't sure how or when to receive it. All I knew to do was to ask the Lord, but was I ready for deliverance? Was I really ready to let go of every one of my selfish and lustful desires of the flesh? Was I ready to walk in holiness with Jesus? Only He could answer those questions, but I was on my knees asking.

I remember asking my roommate, who was also a woman of God, if she had backslid and, just like me, was finding her way back home. She had already been introduced to the things of the Spirit and was filled with the Holy Ghost and fire, which was the evidence of speaking in tongues. She was an interpretative dancer for the Lord. That was one of her gifts. She attended worship service under the ministry of Miracle Life. She could also see visions and had dreams.

When Apostle Collins would pray or speak something over someone, he would blow, and they would fall out by the power of God. It was real and I knew it was confirmation from my Spirit. The Lord let me know Apostle Collins was a man of God and I could trust the Word he was speaking was from God.

I had another dream from the Lord a couple weeks later. I was on my knees and kneeling over a red shiny jewel. I knew the Father was in front of me but I could not look up at Him until He was no longer there, then I looked up and saw what looked like a moon filling up with what resembled little blue squares forming together like puzzle pieces into this circular-shaped moon. Then I yelled up to the sky, "Is it too late?"

I was asking this question to the Lord and all I could see was this beautiful blue sky fade away.

When I told Apostle Collins about this dream, he interpreted: "The red jewel represented the blood of Jesus and the only way to the Father is through the Son."

Finally, I was walking on a straight path. I was praying for deliverance and seeking the Lord.

After a few months, it was like three-and-a-half years into my recovery and this new place in God. I had found the courage to write Rickelle and let go of that part of my life. I told her I wanted to be alone and find who I was in Jesus Christ. I assumed she was okay with it. She never wrote back. She had a boyfriend she was also writing who I knew. We were all friends, so I knew she would be okay.

THE END FROM THE BEGINNING

CHAPTER 18

The Straight Path — Almost

Then here came the enemy to tempt me. He knew my weaknesses — drugs and women. I had all the tools I needed to find sobriety and I was dead set on staying sober. I wanted that more than anything, but I still wasn't delivered from homosexuality. The lustful desires were still there. I was still very attracted to women; I just didn't act on it. I flirted occasionally out of habit. I just couldn't seem to help it.

Deliverance is a process you have to walk out. Everything doesn't happen overnight. Everything doesn't fall off in one day or even a few months.

There was this new girl, Brandi. I didn't even notice her in the beginning, probably because I wasn't really looking. I was trying to stay focused on God, myself, and my sobriety. One of my friends I had met in the program who I worked in housekeeping with told me she had a crush on me. I have to admit I was flattered. I hadn't felt very confident in myself in a long time. I was still very insecure and weak in many areas of my life and this was one of them.

I wanted to be delivered from the principalities and powers of darkness. I wanted to control my sexual passions and destructive behavior, but my flesh was too weak, and we have no power over our flesh. We have to put our flesh under subjection to the will of God under the blood of Jesus. The blood has all power over sin; nothing else. I had to get that revelation before I could actually receive and walk out my deliverance. It is a deeper work of grace. God and only God has the power to purify your heart through and through. He knocks.

Revelation 3:20 (NIV) declares, *"Here I am! I stand at the door and knock. If anyone hears my voice and opens the door, I will come in and eat with that person, and they with me."*

Brandi had someone tell me how she felt and yes, it felt good to be desired. It was hard for me to reject the invitation. I had never turned down an attractive woman who was into me, especially when I was lonely and far away from home with no friends, except for the new ones I had made in the program. The whole situation was still in the front of my mind. I entertained those thoughts for way too long. I would see her and smile, flirting unconsciously and thinking of it consciously in my mind. That was something I still struggled with. Then the moment came where I had a choice to make.

I was standing directly in front of her, knowing how she felt for the most part. I should have steered clear of her and that's it, but my flesh was drawn to her. I asked her how she was doing, and she just came out and said, "I was humiliated. One of your friends told me not to talk to you because you already had a girlfriend so I'm going to just fall back."

The fact that she was up-front honest, and humble enough to tell me she was humiliated allowed me to see her sensitive side, which allowed the enemy to open up a door for it all to go down. I gave her a hug and apologized. She was, as she said, humiliated in front of people. That was the first mistake that I made.

We started having a casual conversation. We were going upstairs, and she took the elevator with me instead of her friends, which was a setup to begin with. As soon as those doors closed, she kissed me and naturally I was shocked and caught off guard and I remember clearly I said, "Whoa, whoa, whoa," in the elevator right in the middle of this kiss.

That was all it took to break the ice and tear down the wall I had tried to create so I wouldn't fall. But eventually I fell. I fell in love with her so fast she had my head spinning. It was too late to turn back now. I had already drunk the kool-aid. I remember those feelings of being wanted and feeling sexy. Those were what I was chasing after. Those were the feelings I was used to. My flesh craved that attention from a woman and, in most cases, women in general.

The Lord offered me a way out. He always does.

The Bible declares, *"No temptation has overtaken you except what is common to mankind. And God is faithful; he will not let you be tempted beyond what you can bear. But when you are tempted, he will also provide a way out so that you can endure it"* (1 Corinthians 10:13, NIV).

He gave me that way out. Instead, I chose her. That was a test and I failed. Deep down I clearly wasn't ready to let go of that sin. It was still in my heart. I wasn't ready for deliverance and that test proved I didn't want to let that go, so I didn't. That warning dream He gave me when He came down on the staircase from heaven shaking his head no — that was for this season. He knew this trap was set for me and I knew where He stood. There was no more doubt, no more excuses. I believed and now knew the truth. We had an understanding.

He clearly said, "No!"

As we started dating, it was like an addiction. All I could do was think about her. All we wanted to do was be together. We were in love, in our own world. After all of the things that God had said and imparted in me, the things of the Spirit I was introduced to, after all the prayers that had been prayed over me. I had found prayer and worship on a whole other level. I had experienced the *dunamis* power of God — dreams, visions, prophecy. I was introduced to the prophetic anointing. He started a work in me. Was it all lost?

The Bible declares (and I am sure of this), *"Being confident of this very thing, that he which haath begun a good work in you will perform it until the day of Jesus Christ"* (Philippians 1:6 KJV).

Looking back, it is now being manifested in my life. I know God is faithful in his Word. Isaiah 55:11 (NIV) says, *"So is my word that goes out of my mouth: It will not return to me empty, but will accomplish what I desire and achieve the purpose for which I sent it."* Amen.

I eventually quit attending Miracle Life and tried to avoid Apostle Collins at all costs. I would always come up with excuses of why I hadn't been coming. I was spending that time with Brandi. I remember when I went to service for the last time. I felt convicted. I felt the power of God. I could now feel the conviction. Before, my heart had been completely hardened and I was comfortable in my sin and I felt extremely uncomfortable in the presence of God. He had begun a work in me. He had softened my heart. I wasn't blind anymore. I could clearly see and feel the sin I was in, and my flesh hated it. I quit reading the Bible. The last Word that God had given me before I started running backwards,

I was running towards Him, toward the kingdom of God. He had straightened my path and put me on the right track. It was my decision to turn back. He gave me this Bible verse one night before I went to sleep and then I could not hear Him anymore.

This is the Word of the Lord that came to me: (Ezekiel 22:2-4a, NIV) *"Son of man, will you judge her? Will you judge this city of bloodshed? Then confront her with all of her detestable practices and say: 'This is what the Sovereign Lord says : You city that brings on herself doom by shedding blood in her midst and defiles herself by making idols, you have become guilty because of the blood you have shed and have become defiled by the idols you have made."*

Ezekiel 22:126, *"And you have forgotten me, declares the Sovereign Lord."*

If that doesn't say it all, I don't know what does. I had turned away from God and He had hidden his face from me. I was scared. I felt like God hated me and I was for sure going to hell. He hated the things I was doing. He hated the way I chose to live again and confronted me — and I was guilty. I didn't open a Bible, I quit going to church, I didn't even pray anymore. I was serving an idol. I made her my God. I chose her. That was one of the worst choices I had ever made.

I ran as far away from God as I could. My life was now going in the direction I was going before. I was sneaking around with her. This was a Christian establishment and I was fornicating every chance I could get. I knew deep down inside if I went back out the devil was going to try and kill me. I was marked. The devil was laughing at me. He was thinking, "I got her now."

God had to hide his face which meant His hands were tied and it was just a matter of time before everything would fall apart just as it did before. Brandi ended up relapsing and was kicked out of the program. I was sneaking around trying to go see her when I was supposed to be working my recovery program and following the rules, getting better. I was worried about her. Soon the enemy was going to use her for me to follow, and I did. Now I was on my own.

Apostle Collins was still praying for me. My family was praying for me. I was no longer under his covering. I was headed for destruction and the enemy wanted me to taste death. My God still loved me. He was still my Savior. Everything that He imparted in me that was Spiritual was still in my heart. The seeds that were sown of the living Word were still in my heart. The enemy cannot steal the seeds that were sewn. He can choke them out, but the seed is forever. The Word is from everlasting to everlasting.

THE END FROM THE BEGINNING

CHAPTER 19

The Beginning: March 3, 2015

The prodigal daughter has returned!

March 3, 2015. That is a day I will never forget.

It was the day the Lord answered every prayer that had been prayed concerning me. As I stepped foot outside, I remember feeling this tingling sensation. I felt good. I remember telling myself, "I feel good about this."

I could feel the power of the hand of God over me as I traveled to my home. I was embarrassed and I knew I looked bad. I was broken into a million pieces. My spirit was dead. There was no hope; there was no light; there was no peace in my eyes. You could see my soul had experienced death. I had tasted death. My heart was broken, and I felt like I could just die.

When I arrived at the bus station on that Greyhound bus my mother was waiting for me. She didn't know what to expect. Neither did I.

I was guilty, full of shame and remorse. I just didn't care anymore. I hated myself. I couldn't stand to look in the mirror. I saw my mom in this beautiful Hyundai Genesis. I hadn't been in a car this nice in a long time. I gave my mother a hug and said, "Hey mom." No excitement in my voice all. You could hear I was in pain.

All I had to my name was a backpack of clothes and the clothes that were on my back.

She was happy to see me. I was surprised at her reaction. All I saw was that big, beautiful Jesus smile of hers and I felt the love that she still had for me. She knew her prayers had been answered. She didn't treat me any different than she had ever treated me before. If anything, she greeted me with open arms. I was accepted just the way I was. The enemy had been whispering lies in my ear, telling me nobody loved me, nobody wanted me, and nobody was going to love me. I was loved by God and my family.

Our first stop was the gas station to get a pack of cigarettes. Mom gave me $20 and we went back to her house. She said, "You hungry?"

I smiled and said, "Yes."

I took a hot bath. I felt like I needed to wash all the filth and sin off of me. I hadn't taken a bath in a long time. The bathroom was immaculate. I felt as if I was in a luxurious hotel, but this was my mother's home. I was finally home!

After I took a bath, mom and Dan had prepared me a home-cooked meal and I just ate my food quietly, thanking them for preparing this meal for me. I talked to them for a while, but I didn't really feel like talking. I was exhausted. My mind was worn down and all I could think about was how I just left Brandi and I was never going back. I had supposedly left for work as usual, but this time I was never coming back.

Mom dropped me off at my sister, Ashley's, and my other sister, Bre, was there. They greeted me with open arms and loved me just the way I was.

I had been on heroin for about a month straight, and all I did that night was cry to my sisters about everything. Bre was sitting next to me on the couch and she consoled me the best she could. My mom had turned off my phone without me even knowing it. I was waiting on Brandi to call, but I didn't need to hear her voice. I knew she would beg me to come back home.

Bre and Ashley were both living for the Lord. They both went to Freedom Life Center Church and were on fire for Jesus. Ashley had given me a Word from the Lord, that I would have three days of grace.

I was like, "What does that mean?"

She said, "I don't know. All He said was three days grace."

The Lord and I hadn't spoken in a long time, but He was in control and in charge of all this. He was healing my mind and my body. I should have had withdrawal from the heroin I was hooked on, but God took it away. That was the grace He was showing me. I had enough on my mind, being sick on top of that. He didn't want that for me. That was a blessing I didn't deserve.

It was snowing and there was like three feet of snow on the ground. I was in and out the back door, smoking cigarettes. I didn't know what to do, what to think. I was at my bottom. I felt as if I didn't have another one in me. I was tired. I couldn't fight anymore.

I couldn't see past my pitiful circumstances, but God saw past all of that and He still had a plan for me. I just didn't know it. I wasn't even looking for Jesus. I thought He hated me and I was doomed. He was certainly looking for me — and He found me.

I started calling homeless shelters because I couldn't stay with my sister. I needed some help. So, by the grace of God, there was a bed for me at the women's YWCA. There was a bed for me on the second floor, which was the floor for homeless and the battered women's program. I thank God. That was another blessing. At that time, I wasn't even counting my blessings. My mind was too messed up for me to even see what was going on around me. Everyone was surprised I got in so quickly. It usually takes six months at least to get in. I took my backpack and a garbage bag full of some clothes and necessities that I would need.

A few more days had gone by. It was Saturday. My mom had my phone turned back on. I told her I needed it. Brandi still had a hold on me, as if she was holding on for dear life. Really it was the devil that had that tight grip and stronghold on me. He just didn't want to let me go. The God I serve had more power and for some reason He still had his hand on me.

Mom came and picked me up. I got in the car and she looked at me and said, "Hi, Kristin."

She did a double take.

I had been sober and, apparently, I looked a little better than I did last time I saw her.

She said, "You look different."

She could see my countenance had changed. I believe the spirit of death was lifted off of me and it showed.

We pulled up at the mall and she didn't say a word. I just followed her, wondering why we were at the mall. We went into a shoe store and she said, "We have to get you some new shoes."

I started jumping up and down, I was so excited. It had been a long time since I had a new pair of shoes. She had bought the ones I had on for me when she and Dan visited me in rehab.

I was now getting settled in the Y. I worked with my dad a little. He let me help him clean a house for

Randy and he gave me some spending money to do it. I remember I met this girl, Natasha. She was also in the program for battered women. She had custody of her two boys at the time, ages 10 and 12. We became friends while we were there. We were allowed to go to the clothing bank and get free clothes, so her and the boys took a little road trip with me and we were able to get some things. I was so thankful. I didn't have any clothes. I felt like we were on a shopping spree. Everything I had been through, the lack and poverty I experienced in Louisville, definitely humbled me and gave me an attitude of gratitude.

I was still struggling in many areas, but I was doing way better than I had in a long time. I was still trying to have a relationship over the phone with Brandi. I kept telling her I would come back, and she would try and make me feel bad for leaving, her telling me I knew I was the only thing she had. The truth of the matter was that soul-tie had to be broken. I was still connected to her and still ridiculously in love with her. This spiritual and emotional connection I still had with her, this particular soul-tie, was destructive and ungodly and had to be broken.

I was going to church on Wednesday nights with my sisters. At first it was just something to do and a free meal, but then it became much more than that. All of us would bring Trisha, who also stayed at the YWCA with me. She also happened to be a close friend I had known ever since I was 17 years old. We had been through a lot together, struggling with drugs and alcohol. Trisha and I knew the worst of each other and had always been all about drugs. Our friendship revolved around the meth we were doing, and we would always team up and do whatever we had to do to get it. Trisha is one of the only women that I was friends with who I didn't sleep with. We were in a lot of sexual situations, but we were never directly intimate with each other.

I was still doing pills here and there, whenever I could get hold of some. I also drank a few times, but I wasn't able to catch any kind of buzz off of either. In fact, it made me sick the next day. I thought it was because I was so used to hard drugs this stuff just wasn't potent enough.

I then decided I had to get a job. I was tired of sitting in that place all day, bored out of my mind, not able to get high - nothing. My friend Trisha worked at Residence Inn and told me Hampton was right across the street and that they were hiring. I got some bus tokens from my counselor and went to the Hampton Inn. I felt very insecure and had such an inferiority complex from past experiences, consistently failing at everything that I set out to do. I had a black Carhartt jacket with a hole in the bottom of my right sleeve which had the cotton hanging out of it. I tried to cover it up so I wouldn't look homeless, in fear that I might not get the job. I was hired that day — another blessing from the Lord. I wasn't able to start right away. I had to get an ID from the license branch. This time I was able to get all the documents I needed to receive one.

20

CHAPTER 20

A Strong Foundation

Everything was just falling into place. I was in this constant flow of grace and mercy. I was starting to gain some self-confidence. I had a safe place to stay with everything I needed and now a job. Things were definitely looking up for me. The grace of God was all over me. I wasn't sure why, but I continued to move forward, expecting something to go wrong and eventually fall apart just as it always had.

But not this time. There was something different about this time around. What was it?

Could it have been the impartation and visitation from the Lord I had experienced three years prior while

I was under the ministry of Apostle Collins? Could it have been the simple fact that the Lord had come to me in a dream and I had seen His face?

Genesis 32:30 NIV, when Jacob wrestled with God, says, *"So Jacob called the place Peniel* [which means the face of God] *saying, 'It is because I saw God face to face, and yet my life was spared.'"* It is because I saw the face of God in a dream. Therefore, no matter what I went through, how far away from God I was, even tasting death, the grave could not hold me because the Lord had spared my life.

That day I went back to the YWCA with a good job. I was used to making next to nothing in Louisville and working like a slave dog and having absolutely nothing to show for it. This housekeeping job started out at $7.25 an hour. I was blessed and so grateful for a real job. I called my sister, Bre. She was on drug court at the time and her story was my story. She was also looking for a job, so she went out there and they offered her a job at Residence Inn right across the street. We were able to ride to work together every morning. She had to check in at Boonville in the mornings before work by 8 a.m., which gave us about an hour to rebuild our relationship. We were both chasing after Jesus, so all we did was worship and talk about the things of God. We both grew so much in our walk and fed that fire with praise and worship. God was finishing the work He had started in us both.

I then started attending church and Bible study faithfully. The Holy Spirit allowed me to see that I had to let go of Brandi. We were still talking on the phone as if we were working on our relationship and I was going to go back to her after I saved some money. I had too much to lose now. I was starting to be happy and feel again. That darkness had begun to lift from me and things were actually going good for the first time in many years. I couldn't remember the last time I felt happy. My worst day now was better than my best day before. Was God really changing me? Is there really a happy ending? I thought, "Okay, slow down, just take it one day at a time." I didn't want to put any expectations on myself and be disappointed because I never succeed or do well at anything I do.

Bre was working the A.A. program faithfully and I decided to go with her. Why not? I didn't have anything else better to do. We went a few times a week and we would go around the room and have an open discussion. I would always pass, but Bre would always share. I remember her saying how it was a miracle that I was sitting next to her in the rooms at A.A.

"An answered prayer," is what she said.

That's when I realized God is real. These A.A. people are real. It really does work if you work it.

I finally got a revelation that a power higher than myself could restore me back to sanity, and that power was the blood of Jesus Christ.

Bre had quit talking to her girlfriend and let go of that sin. I knew it was time for me to do the same.

Then I realized: How was I going to do this? I had been trapped and entangled in this sin for so long time I didn't know how to get out. We started attending this Bible study on Wednesday nights. It was a group of new believers who had been set free from addictions and every other demonic stronghold they were bound in. Our teacher was Alice Gates, a mighty woman of God who walked and lived a very righteous life. The Lord had sent her to Freedom for us, to teach us "Foundations." That was the book we were taught out of from in the beginning of our walk. She actually took me to the mall and bought me some clothes. She would always come up behind me when I went up for prayer, every single time.

I looked at her like: "What is this 60-year-old lady doing taking an interest in me, trying to be my friend?" I thought it was weird, but little did I know I had been assigned to her by God. He put her in my path to mentor me and all the others in this foundations class.

I was starting to ask questions and had a desire to learn the Bible and wanted a closer walk with Him. This church stuff was working, and I wanted to figure it out. Alice took a special interest in me for some reason, and she was in awe, noticing the transformation that was taking place in, on, and around me. I went to Bible study with my friend, Trisha, who was also living at the

YWCA and trying to stay sober. She started to see the change in me and also came to Bible study with me and Bre. She worked at the Residence Inn with Bre. We were all on the same path. I went to Alice one Wednesday night and I told her, "I can't stop calling Brandi. She has a hold on me and I can't let go."

THE END FROM THE BEGINNING

CHAPTER 21

True Liberty

Alice said, "That's because you have to break that soul-tie," which is that spiritual and emotional connection you have when you are intimate with someone. In this case this was an ungodly soul-tie that needed to be broken in order for me to be loosed.

I asked her how to do that. She said I needed deliverance and deliverance ministry is one of the gifts and callings that the Lord had given her. So, with Trisha in the room I said, "Let's do it now."

I sat across from Alice and she looked me directly in my eyes and called that demon out as I repeated after her a prayer to be loosed. I had tears streaming down my face. I sincerely, in my heart, wanted the power of deliverance. Now I was ready to let that sin go, and God knew it.

I received deliverance immediately after that prayer.

The next morning, I called my mom and I asked her to turn off my phone and change my number. She asked me why, and I said, "Long story, but I will pay for it."

I then erased every picture I had in my phone of Brandi. I had looked at her pictures every night before I went to sleep. I had to close my eyes as I erased them in my mind. I knew I was set free after I did that. The Bible declares in John 8:36 (NIV), *"So if the Son sets you free, you will be free indeed."*

After that I was off and running relentlessly towards Jesus. My chains were finally broken by the power of God. I decided I wasn't going to do pills anymore. I wanted to live for Jesus. I decided that I wanted to get baptized again and give my life to the Lord again and start all over. I felt the Holy Spirit tugging on my heart to be baptized again, so I did.

On May 3, 2015, my sister, Bre, and I were both baptized and reborn again at Freedom Life Center. When I was immersed in the water of our baptismal tank in the name of the Father, the Son, and the Holy Spirit, I was born into a new life with Jesus. I didn't "feel" the power of God; lightning didn't strike; but I was changed forever. I felt whole. I felt free, really free for the first time in my entire life. I began to walk, talk, and think differently. Everything around me changed. Even every aspect of circumstances changed. I was on fire and full of so much joy every day. I felt better than any drug or drink ever made me feel. This was a different kind of high. There is no high like the most-high God.

I continued to save all my money. I gave it to my mother for safekeeping and I tithed faithfully. I had always tried to give a little to church when I was in Louisville under Apostle Collins' ministry, trying to still feel some sort of connection with what I had found spiritually. I later learned that God doesn't want your money, He wants your heart, which is an acceptable sacrifice to Him. The importance of tithing is giving God what is His. He is the One who gave it to you and 10% of everything He blesses you with belongs to the kingdom of God and the ministry you are under. The Bible says in Leviticus 27:30 (NIV), *"A tithe of everything from the land, whether grain from the soil or fruit from the trees, belongs to the Lord; it is holy to the Lord."*

When you don't, it is also breaking the spiritual law of prosperity. Luke 6:38 (KJV) says, *"Give, and it shall be given unto you; good measure, pressed down, shaken together, and running over, shall men give unto your bosom. For with the same measure ... it shall be measured to you."*

I know giving my tithe to the Lord is a covenant that is made between me and Him, in knowing He will provide everything I need always. He is faithful and always has been, even when I was not.

I was still working at the Hampton, living at the YWCA, which is considered a homeless shelter. I tithed and I was blessed. I was now ministering to the girls in the program and testifying about what the Lord had done for me, I even led a Bible study for all the women on the importance of the Ten Commandments and what they represented, how I was living for Jesus and everything had turned around. God works all things out for the good of those who love Him and are called according to His purpose.

I had a roommate named Jennifer at the Y. We became close. I shared Jesus with her and always took her to Bible study with me. She held me accountable as far as work was concerned. Jennifer was a hard worker and never called in. There would be mornings I wasn't feeling it and wanted to stay in bed, but she would motivate me and say, "Come on Kristin, let's roll." I appreciated that. We worked side by side and worked as a team. She was my road dog and was a very good friend.

My dad had a 2011 Chevy Malibu that he had bought for his ex-wife. In the middle of a divorce he had the idea he would have me take over the payments to prevent a repossession. I had money saved and I was also getting my driver's license online. It had been suspended for 12 years and I never had the unction to try and get it back. I figured there was no point, since I didn't have a vehicle and I couldn't even see myself with one. I had one car when I was 18 years old that my mother co-signed for me and it was repossessed before I even had it six months. It was a failure I still carried with me. My dad told me I could come pick up the car if I took over the payments.

I asked my mom and Dan what they thought about it and they said I shouldn't because I didn't make enough income to afford it, which was the truth. I only made $7.25 an hour and averaged a little over $500 every 2 weeks, but I was determined I was going to take over the payments. So, I did. I gave him $364.00 for the first month and my roomy, Jennifer, drove me to Granny's and I left with it, feeling like I was on top of the world. My dad said the insurance was taken care of, so in my mind I was going to work all the overtime I could get to afford this car. It was a beautiful pearl full-sized luxury car with 18-inch silver chrome rims. I was doing the most! I was truly blessed. I had a job, a car, and I was sober, living for Jesus. How much better could things get? I had never had it this good. Life was never this great. This living for Jesus thing was phenomenal.

I started working 25 hours of overtime every pay period which was bringing home a little over $750 bi-weekly. As soon as that car payment was due, I drove that $364 straight to my dad. I had experienced the heartbreak of one car possession years ago, I was not going to ever let that happen again. Then something else miraculous happened. I heard SMC, a contracting company, was hiring through Toyota — a job I always dreamed of having. I had applied there when I was 18 years of age before drugs and alcohol were a part of my story and I didn't make the cut. I called and set up an interview.

By the grace of God, His hand was on my life. I had been baptized with water and resurrected, which helped me realize that God is needed for salvation from sin — going under, dying in my old way of life, and rising from the water with a new life of salvation. I immediately knew in my spirit that life would never be as I had known it before. A life full of nothing but failure after failure and disappointment so deeply rooted I was afraid to try. I was afraid to put expectations on myself and go through the agony of defeat. But this was different. These expectations were not of my own, but expectations of God's power.

I knew I couldn't do this on my own. The Lord gave me a Word that dropped in my spirit: "I will not let you fail."

I immediately received that revelation and, once I realized it wasn't me but the power of God that was going to lead and guide me through this, I was then able to put Kristin to the side and give Jesus the wheel. I was an empty vessel, available and ready to be used by God. I wasn't afraid anymore.

There was something more God wanted me to have — a deeper level in Him. I had this desire to speak in tongues. It was a heavenly language and a gift that I wanted. Ashley and Bre had already been given the gift of tongues. I wanted that gift too. I received prayer every church service and at every revival. I asked for the gift of tongues every time I went to the altar. Why wasn't I able to receive that gift? Was I not holy enough? Was I overthinking it? Yes! It wasn't in my mind - it had to come from within. Tongues is a gift of the Spirit that can only come from God to those who believe. The Spirit of the living God falls, and you are baptized with fire, resulting in the evidence of speaking in tongues.

Acts 1:5,8 (NKJV) says, *"For John truly baptized with water, but you shall be baptized with the Holy Spirit not many days from now... But you shall receive power when the Holy Spirit has come upon you; and you shall be witnesses to Me in Jerusalem, and in all Judea and Samaria, and to the end of the earth."*

After many prayers, I remember the whole church came up to me and laid hands on me, hoping to help me receive, which some do. Right there at the altar I have seen people break out in tongues after prayer. But for me it was different — more simplified, I guess you could say. I was at home praying in the middle of the floor with my sister, Bre.

She said, "Let's ask God to baptize you with fire," so we did. My sister then put her hand over my stomach as my hands were reaching for the sky and she was praying in the Spirit. I was still overthinking it.

Then all of a sudden, I said, "I'm going to sing it," then I started singing in the Spirit. Then we both started busted up laughing. All you heard was four simple syllables, so, le, la, ten. All it took was faith and God gave me the gift of tongues that day — just me and my sister in the presence of God in the middle of our living room. I sang in the Spirit every day after that. I was so thankful. Eventually I learned how to also pray in the Spirit, which is my direct line to the Father at any given time in any moment.

There was another God-encounter me and my sister had not long after that one. We were in the prayer closet and Bre had a Word from the Lord for me. I knew it was truth. I could always feel it in my Spirit and a witness I would get confirming I was hearing from the Lord. She placed her hand on my heart and the Lord said he had given me a new heart, which I received by faith that day.

Ezekiel 36:26 (NIV) says, *"I will give you a new heart and put a new spirit in you; I will remove from you your heart of stone and give you a heart of flesh."*

This heart that I was now operating out of was pure. I was able to walk in purity and love others with the love of God, walking in the Spirit — the Holy Spirit — who lives inside of me.

The unthinkable happened. My dad was going through a lot with his previous divorce and my Granny was sick. He would borrow the car on the weekends to take Granny back and forth to the hospital. She had dementia and was dying.

My dad had recently quit his job to take care of Granny and, even though I was making the car payments to him, somehow he managed to get behind and the car was being repossessed. There was nothing I could do about it. The car was in his name and our deal was I was going to take over the loan.

Granny died and my dad got even further behind. I had saved up $1,000. I gave it to Mom to hold and I was prepared to go to the bank and take over. But they would not let me take over the loan. It was going to be repossessed. I was heartbroken. I knew I had to give the car back. I loved that car. That was the only thing I had that made me feel like I was getting somewhere, like I had something to show for me being used to having nothing of value.

The truth is, that car did not define me. What I had to hold on to was way more valuable than earthly possessions. I knew who I was in Christ and what He has for me is for me. Any door He opens man can shut.

Revelation 3:7 (NIV) says, *"These are the words of him who is holy and true, who holds the key of David. What he opens no one can shut, and what he shuts no one can open. I know your deeds. See, I have placed before you an open door that no one can shut. I know that you have little strength, yet you have kept my word and have not denied my name."*

This situation was also a test.

I could have been depressed, blamed God for taking away from me that car I loved. I could have gone back to my old ways and got totally wasted. It looked like I was losing my car. How was I going to get back and forth to work every day? My faith was being tested.

I decided to get on my knees and pray. I had learned in this walk of faith that my praise is my weapon, so I was going to trust and believe what the Bible says. Romans 8:28 (NIV): *"And we know that in all things God works for the good of those who love him, who have been called according to his purpose."*

I was learning to live by faith, not by sight and God was working behind the scenes for my good.

My sister, Erica, had applied for Aerotek a couple of months prior to me starting. It was around October. By the grace of God, Erica just happened to start work that following Monday for Aerotech. I had just moved in with her and Bre in this one-bedroom apartment, but we were all sober and we all had jobs. We were able to ride to work together in the mornings.

I remember Mom told me to drop the car off at the bank in Newburgh and have my dad pick it up from there, since they would not allow me to take over the loan and it was not in my name. Therefore, it wasn't okay for me to drive it and I did as she asked. I knew it was the right thing to do, so I did.

I was on my way home with Erica on a Sunday afternoon after dropping off the car. I called Mom and said, "It's done."

She asked me, "Do you want me to take you to Henderson Chevrolet next weekend to look at cars?"

I said, " Yea."

I was a little sad and disappointed, but I was going to make the best of this situation. So, I went to work the next morning, praising the Lord, believing He would turn it all around.

One evening I was having a conversation with my sister, Bre, and she said, "Kristin, God is going to bless you with a better car and the payments will be lower."

I gave her a smile and answered, "I hope so."

She said, "I'm prophesying over you and you don't even know it."

The very next Saturday, Mom did what she said she would do. She was being led by the Holy Spirit. She wasn't even sure at the time why we were going, but God knew. Mom, Erica and me drove to Henderson and pulled in the parking lot. I remember Mom putting on her lipstick before we got out of the car and some young gentleman came up to the car. It was the same guy that sold Mom the car that Erica was driving a couple years back. When he came up to the car, she told him we were just looking and she would come find him if we needed help. In other words, leave us alone — I'll come find you if we need you, so he left.

We were browsing in the used car section. I was dead set that the only car I wanted was a 2011 Chevy Malibu, which is what I just had, but they had none. Mom was looking at a white 2014 Hyundai Sonata. Some older gentleman, a car salesman, was standing by my mom and asked her if she liked it. He then said, "Let me see how much that one is," so he came out and told us that $17,995 was the asking price.

Mom said, "Well, let's see if you can get approved before we look at anything."

She made it very clear she was not going to co-sign, and she wanted to get my credit established. I was completely unprepared. I wasn't sure what we were even doing to begin with. If Mom wasn't co-signing, then it's a wrap.

I didn't have a driver's license with me, absolutely nothing. He asked me how long I had been at Toyota, which was only a few months. All I had was a brand-new savings account so my check could be directly deposited. My credit was horrible. He wrote down all of my personal and financial information and went to see what he could do.

Mom was getting restless and she was ready to go home. Things weren't looking good anyway. He came back and said I can't do anything without a co-signer. Mom said no, so he went back to the back again.

Mom was tired of waiting, so she said, "Let's go. This is pointless."

My hopes of getting a car were crushed. We all got in Mom's Cadillac and started to drive off.

I remember Mom telling me, "Now I told you we were just coming to look."

The guy we were dealing with had seen the disappointment on my face. Suddenly he came running to the window and knocked as we were pulling off. "I got you the deal! I got you the deal!"

I frantically said, "Mom, can we go see?" So, we all got out of the car and started to negotiate. He said, "I can get it in your name for $15,995, but you have to have a down payment. Can you afford $3,000?"

I said, "No, I can afford $2,000."

This was the Holy Spirit speaking through me. The Lord obviously had a hand in this. Mom had $1000 cash of mine in her bank account. I had her hold on to for me and I was about to get paid another $800 paycheck, so I said, "Mom, will you loan me $1000? She said okay. He told me all I needed was a check dated 30 days from now for $2,000. Before I could even get out of my mouth that I didn't have a checking account, Mom said, "I'll write the check and she can just pay me back."

Next thing you know, I was leaving in a 2014 Hyundai Sonata and a $318 car payment in my name. I didn't have anything when I walked on that car lot, not a paystub or even a driver's license and God made a way out of no way. I have tasted and seen that the Lord is good, blessed, and highly favored.

I was determined to allow God to fulfill His plan and His purpose He had given me before the foundations of the earth were laid. I was full of unspeakable joy every day. I was now addicted to the Word of God rather than the things of this world. All of the desires of my flesh that once ruled over me were gone. He had changed the desires of my heart. I was no longer a slave to sin. I got up in the mornings and thanked the Lord for another day. These days were ones I could look forward to.

I would show up for work at Toyota every morning with my Jesus smile and believed God would get me through the day, and He always did.

I struggled a lot. I had never been expected to perform on a level this high. I never had a real job. I never held a job over a year and the work I had done wasn't complex. I had no work ethic, no work experience, yet I was determined I was going to make it through at one of the most prestigious motor manufacturing companies in the world.

I couldn't help but beat myself up from time to time because I was struggling to learn the processes I was training in. I knew if I didn't get it, I would eventually be fired. I went home crying a lot of days, feeling less-than and also inadequate. I felt as if maybe I wasn't smart enough, maybe the effect of the drugs and alcohol prevented me from being able to function on a high level or excel in life. The fact that I never made it past my sophomore year in high school certainly didn't help things. I had always failed in school to the point where I quit trying. But it was all taken care of at the cross.

The Bible clearly states in 2 Timothy 1:7 (NKJV), *"For*

God has not given us a spirit of fear; but of power, and of love, and of a sound mind."

After many years of wrong thinking and destructive behavior, it's a process. The transformation of our mind, renewing it daily, is something we have to choose to do and believe one day at a time.

I finally was given the job of pushcart, which was a repetitive job, but that's how I was able to learn. I knew without a shadow of a doubt that God had my group leader to be Candace. She was my work mentor. She was a hard worker and had so much patience with me. I remember I would forget something almost every morning. If it wasn't my gloves it was my safety glasses, my hard hat, or my pouch. I was completely irresponsible, but I gave it my all and she knew that. If it had been anyone else, I would have been let go.

The struggle was real but Candace was determined to get me to the place I needed to be to succeed. No matter what, that woman would not give up on me. She never yelled at me or made me feel stupid. She would just give me this beautiful smile and I would instantly calm down and start all over again.

I loved Candace. She had a great heart and she was for me. I would have never gotten to the place I needed to be if God hadn't have used her to be an influence in my life. I remember she shared some things with me about her personal life and the Lord asked me to pray with her. I was terrified of what she might think. She was my boss and I figured she would think I was weird.

I remember telling her one day at end shift, "The Lord wants me to pray with you."

She smiled and we would pray. She then told me that her parents were super Christians, so I knew that's was how she was raised, and she was a believer. I had such an inferiority complex. I only prayed with her because the Lord asked me to, which now I saw why.

Candace was a go-getter. She showed up to work every day. She always handled herself in a professional manner. I wanted to be just like her. She was very intelligent and went over and beyond her job duties, which was why she had already been promoted three times from team member to team leader — and now my group leader. She didn't seem like she ever struggled. I asked her questions and shared my work struggles with her and she would always tell me, "This is five years of experience, Kristin. You'll get there."

She was always encouraging me, which is why I was so inspired by her.

I continued to make it to Bible study every Wednesday. I couldn't wait to tell everyone how God did it again. Alice was in awe. She used to be this old lady I wished would stop following me around every time I would go up for prayer. I would look back and there was Alice. She was now much more than that. She was a mighty woman of God who had been sent from God as an assignment to teach and guide us in the right direction. She was my mentor. I called her every day for prayer and, just like a babe in Christ, I always had questions. I was on fire for Jesus and she was my biggest fan. She loved me and I was her favorite for some reason. Quite frankly, she was mine. Everyone is entitled to have a favorite and I really needed the love of God and extra attention she showed me. I was so broken and had no self-esteem. The confidence I may have once had decades ago she helped me with. She would always tell me how proud she was of me and how she was blessed to see the work that God had done in me. She had become one of my closest friends.

I now had a life that was spiritual and structured. I went to work every day. My work week consisted of anywhere from 50-55 hours a week. We worked a lot of overtime, which was good for me. I didn't have time to get into trouble. I was too worn out during the week to even think about anything other than getting up at 4:15 every morning, driving 40 minutes to Princeton, and then getting off at 5:15 p.m., getting home around 6 p.m., and doing it all over again. This was exactly what I needed. I took my job very seriously. I wasn't sure how long I was going to last. My goal was to work directly for Toyota and eventually retire from there.

One morning I was on my way to work, driving down Highway 41, listening to my worship. I wasn't paying attention and ran into the truck in front of me. It was a fender bender, but I was very upset. Luckily I had good insurance and they gave me a check for $1000. I had to come up with the other $500 deductible. I couldn't stand my car being wrecked. It was brand new and I wanted it fixed immediately. I had to finish paying Mom off for the down payment and also had to make sure I had my car payment every month, so I was going to have to wait until I got my taxes or something before I was able to come up with the deductible.

Erica was behind in rent and had been long before I came around. We were going to have to move soon out of that one-bedroom apartment, so I prayed to the Lord and He told me to start looking for an apartment.

I didn't know where to start, so I said, "Where do I start, Lord?"

I bought a newspaper after work one night and was going to look in the ads for apartments for rent. I took a shower, had a fresh hot Little Caesars pizza, and called the first apartment I saw. I gave the lady my information and she said she would get back with me. I wasn't in any hurry. I really didn't know what to expect. I thought this was going to be a long process.

She called me two days later and said I could move in. I was shocked. Could this really be happening? Me, having my own place? I had never had my own place before. I told her I hadn't even started packing yet. I had a paycheck on the way and a $1,000 insurance check. I called Mom to ask her if I could use the insurance check since it was made out to me, and I was going to get my car fixed when I got my taxes. So, I took Mom with me that weekend and I took my own money and got an apartment for me, Erica, and Bre to move into. I was so blessed! Another blessing from the Lord.

I dedicated my home to the Lord, and I proclaimed Joshua 24:15 (NIV): *"But as for me and my household, we will serve the Lord."*

I couldn't even begin to wrap my mind around the transformation that was going on in my life. Only one year prior, I had only one backpack to my name and was living in a homeless shelter, with no job, no money, and trapped in addiction. No one wanted to be around someone who was full of hurt and pain, with nothing going for them, nothing to give. At that time, I couldn't even hide my brokenness inside. It was written all over my face.

Now, only a year later, I hold with my head high with a beautiful Jesus smile that lights up every room I step into. I'm now walking in the authority and power that was given to me by God. My countenance has changed so much, to the point I am hardly recognizable to those who knew me a year prior. This light in my eyes I've never had before, not even as a child.

I had my own place that the Lord had blessed me with for me and my family. I had a driver's license for the first time in 22 years, a good job that I loved, and a brand-new car that was in my name. How is this even humanly possible? It is not. Only the grace and favor of

God could turn this lost and blind sinner into a Mighty Princess Warrior of God.

The days, weeks, and months went by and I continued to serve the Lord. I always shared with any and everyone in my path what the Lord had done for me, that if He would do it for me then He would do it for them. It was 2016 and I was still on fire for Jesus. It was almost Christmastime. My sister, Erica, no longer worked at Toyota but I was still holding on.

It was hard. They had done away with my job and built the Dragon. I wasn't trained in anything else and every other process I tried I failed. They put me right back on pushcart. I then started training to learn floor wire. It was in the same area I was already in so it was either shape up or ship out. To be honest I gave it everything I had every day, but I still couldn't get this job down.

The team members were starting to make fun of me and trying to intimidate me. They made fun of me because I was a Christian and they tried to push my buttons just to see if I would cuss them out. They had never heard me say a cuss word and they weren't going to either.

I went home crying every day asking the Lord to help me, just to help me learn this job like everyone else.

Why was everything always so hard for me? Why was I the only one who just couldn't get it? What was wrong with me? Everyone around me thought I was an idiot and I couldn't learn this job. Candace reprimanded me almost every day. She never yelled at me. She just told me I couldn't have any more quality issues. I was in training for four months. Another team leader had to check everything before I could send it out. Candace said she was keeping me in it until I got it. She was the only one who had faith in me.

I didn't even believe in myself. I knew God was capable of making me good at this. I was going through it every single day. I would be at church on Sundays, lying on the altar, crying out to the Lord to help me. I would pray every morning with Joey, my spiritual dad, and he would encourage me and told me I had to walk through what the Lord wanted me to walk through and, no matter what, I couldn't give up. I had failed so many times. Success was the only thing that mattered. I was going to master this and become one of the best.

Ten hours a day in a nonstop process was definitely a challenge for me, but the Lord was teaching me perseverance and the motivation I would need to succeed in life. I had to learn to keep on going in to face the setbacks and every challenge I would come against.

I would tell myself every day my favorite scripture, Matthew 6:33 (KJV): *"But seek ye first the kingdom of God, and his righteousness; and all these things shall be added unto you."*

I knew if I just continued to put one foot in front of the other and seek God, he would handle the rest. I knew that I couldn't hold this job on my own, pay my bills, and be financially responsible. I'd never done or even been close to having a structured life like everyone else. All I knew how to do was pray and give it to God and I did. He has been my provider and I haven't lost anything He has blessed me with. His Word is truth, and he has been faithful.

The Lord started to give me dreams. I hadn't had any dreams from God since 2012 when I was in Louisville under Apostle Collins' ministry. I was now walking in the things of the Spirit and experiencing dreams and visions again.

The dream I had in 2016 I wrote down in what I call my dream book. Every dream from the Lord I write down. Most of them I don't have an interpretation for yet. With a few, I called a couple of men of God who operate in interpretation, including Apostle Collins.

In this dream, my mom and I were in her white Mercedes. She was driving and I was in the front passenger side. I felt like my sisters were all in the back. We were driving down the road and this black lady was standing in the middle of the street. Cars were passing by. It was as if she was waiting for us. She had a long, sleeveless, gold, V-neck dress on. She was brown skinned. The length of her hair was to her shoulders. The woman made eye contact with us and walked up to the car holding a baby. Mom and I knew she was trying to give away her baby. It seemed as if she didn't really want to give it away and she seemed sad about it.

She said, "Will you hold my baby for a minute?"

She was looking at my mom and handed the baby through the driver's side window. Mom took the baby and the lady slowly walked backwards and disappeared. Mom had the baby in her lap while driving, holding it on her left leg.

I said, "We gotta go find the lady!"

So, we drove around and I said realizing, "We are not going to find her."

Then all of a sudden I was sitting on my bed holding the baby all by myself. Bre tried to walk in, slowly cracking the door open. I said I was blessing the baby. I was looking at this baby with love and compassion, wondering why the baby's mother just left.

Approximately five months later, I found out Erica was pregnant and Malichi, my nephew, was born that year — December 26, 2016. I'd had a dream of Malichi before he was even born. The lady in my dream that gave us the baby represented the angel of the Lord.

It was so good to be able to enjoy the holidays with my family. I was now able to buy everyone real Christmas presents. I never had a steady job and was able to bless my family in that way, instead of the home-made cards I had been giving my mother for the past 20 years. I was able to give instead of just receive. On New Year's Eve, we closed the church down. We had a New Year's Eve worship service. I had never spent New Year's in church. In the past, I was always high and drunk, out clubbing all night. Now I partied in the Lord.

I get excited about the things of God and am happier now than I have ever been. Who would have thought living for Jesus would be fun? I have so much peace, laying my head down at night knowing my heart is right with God. It is a good feeling knowing that you know that you know that you know your name is written in the Lamb's Book of Life. I can honestly say if Jesus came right now, I'm ready. I have completely surrendered my will to God and given myself to Him.

By the grace of God, I don't struggle with craving sex from women and needing to be validated by someone else to feel loved. I feel loved. I feel the love of God in my heart and my Spirit. I had never been able to control my lustful desires prior to this, but now God had given me the gift of celibacy.

I had a ring I was saving for my girlfriend. It was a beautiful sterling silver ring donated to the YWCA and awarded to me; I was able to pick out two of them for doing extra chores. After my change of heart, I decided to give one to my sister, Erica, and the other one I dedicated to the Lord and put on my right ring finger to show my faithfulness to Him.

I have given my heart to Jesus and in return He has given me His heart. His heart is pure, and I am able to love others from a pure heart with *agape*, which is the highest form of love — the love of God for man and of man for God.

During this time, the Lord put it in my heart to write a book, a book about my walk with Him and how I have overcome. This had to be in the distant future because I had no idea how I could write a book. I was a high school dropout and I've done way too many drugs. The education I did have was lost from my drug use.

In 2017 my baby sister, Bre, who lived with me at the time, was married and had a beautiful baby girl, Mia. Erica and Bre seemed to always do everything together their entire childhood. Being one year apart in age, they have always been very close. Now they were going to be raising children together. Bre then moved out and Erica and Malichi moved in. What a blessing. I used to not really be a kid person, but I love my nieces and nephews to death. I never knew kids could be so much fun. I myself have no desire to have kids and I never have.

Now that I am sober and living for Jesus I am focused on the purpose and the plan Jesus has for my life. My passion is to help those who are struggling in addiction and sin, through implementing change, by pouring what has been poured into me — the Word of God. I have come so far, and I haven't even really begun to see everything the Lord has for me. I have grown much. All these years of hard work will pay off. I know God is just preparing me for what is to come. Hitting the pavement every day, showing up, giving it all I got, and encouraging others around me — that's what I'm meant to do.

I was created to walk in love and share the good news.

My spiritual mother and mentor was diagnosed with cancer that year and, by the end of the year after a good fight, she received her miracle and went to be with Jesus. She never lost her faith and never stopped believing God. It was hard but I knew how much she loved Jesus and I learned so much from her and all that praying she was doing for me sure paid off.

Later that year after a couple of minor injuries, I tore a muscle in my back and was in pain for months. I was off work recovering for a few weeks with no pay and I didn't know how I was going to make ends meet. I struggled financially. I had lived from paycheck to paycheck ever since I started, but I had remained faithful in my tithes and the Lord had given me everything I needed.

CHAPTER 22

Double For My Trouble

Money has always been tight, but God has always made a way. Everything the enemy stole from me, God has given me double for my trouble.

God says in His Word that you will receive double for your trouble. God is faithful and I believe every word.

This scripture the Lord gave me when I first started this journey with Him was Isaiah 61:7 (NKJV): *"Instead of your shame you shall have double honor, and instead of confusion they shall rejoice in their portion. Therefore, in their land they shall possess double; everlasting joy shall be theirs."*

I was honored in December 2017 as "Team Member of the Month"! West Plant Blue Final for overall Performance, Quality, Safety, and Attendance. I was so proud of that and it was worth it. That gave me the self-confidence I needed to keep going.

The year 2018 was tough for me. I struggled at work. Physically the job I had was indeed very strenuous. I would go home crying almost every night, praying that the Lord would help me through and bless me with a promotion. I received a prophetic word, "Promotion," and I had been praying for it ever since 2016. I would always tell my friends and my sisters to be specific in prayer, so I prayed the Lord would bless me with an office job where I could look out at a beautiful view.

I said, "When — not if, but when — the Lord blesses me, I'm going to sit in my chair in my office and prop my feet up and cross my legs and admire this beautiful view I have."

I was speaking it into existence.

The Lord had put it on my heart to start taking classes at night for my GED. A door just opened and I began taking classes at St. Lucas Church in Evansville. It was three nights a week from 4:30 to 7:30 p.m. and they would work around my work schedule.

I had to commute from Princeton which was a 45-minute drive and wouldn't get started until 6:30. I was completely exhausted and had a long way to go. I never made it past the tenth grade and this mission seemed impossible, but the Lord put it on my heart so He would see me through. My faith was really being tested. A family friend that had known my mother for years, Billy Garrett, had been attending classes at Ivy Tech through WorkOne and referred me there. I went twice and tested to see where I was academically and what it was going to take for me to reach my goal. I showed up one Monday night and no one was there. Our teacher had been transferred and I was lost in the shuffle. It was about three weeks before I decided to try and see what was going on.

I was then moved to night classes at Memorial Baptist Church, which was right down the street from my house. My very first night I met Ms. Rhonda, a God-fearing woman. Her passion was to help us achieve our goal, no matter the cost. I knew God had put her in my path to help me along the way.

I tested all over again to see where I was academically, and I was at a fourth and fifth grade level in every subject. I was so embarrassed. I couldn't believe how behind I really was. This mission now seemed impossible. I had to make up seven to eight years of education before I could even be on a high school level.

I started to cry, but then Ms. Rhonda said, "You are where you are. You can't change that. We have work to do but you can do it."

I then started to think, "Well if she thinks it can be done then maybe I have a chance."

I knew that only God could get me through this. If He brought me out of addiction and all the darkness I was once in, surely He could do this too. It was going to take a lot of work, but I was willing. At first, I was super motivated but then the new wore off and I hardly ever felt like going. There were times when all I could do was show up. My mind was too exhausted to retain anything. I didn't feel like I was getting anywhere.

Ms. Rhonda and I became really close friends. She was like me. She loved to talk about Jesus. She sang in the choir at Memorial and her faith inspired me. The fact that she was always encouraging me helped. No matter what, I wasn't giving up, even if it took me five years. The Lord gave me a promise. He said He would not let me fail and I was trusting in that.

It usually took students anywhere from six months to a year to graduate. I had been out of school so long I couldn't even remember how to work simple fractions and my reading and language had to improve dramatically. I started reading the Bible even more and a lot of Christian literature — T.D. Jakes, Joyce Meyer. Anything I thought could get me where I needed to be, I read. I was also trying to start writing this book the Lord had put on my heart to share about my testimony and how the Lord has brought me completely out of darkness. I was thinking, "How can someone reading and writing at a fifth-grade level even think about writing a book?"

I prayed the Lord would help me get where I needed to be, but I just felt like I was too far behind. Everyone else around me started testing and I procrastinated because I didn't feel like I was making any progress. I didn't feel any smarter. The year was almost over, and I was still showing up, still working out of the workbooks, trying to get through. Then 2019 came around. Life was still the same, working at Toyota, still on fire for Jesus.

Then on April 18, 2019, I was at work picking floor wire, just about to take lunch. Lunch was at 10:30. Exactly two minutes before lunch, as I was scanning a piece of floor wire, I dropped my scanner on my right foot. I didn't have my composite toe shoes on that day. I had just bought a pair of new work shoes and was trying to break them in. I had blisters on my feet. That day of all days I had the wrong shoes on, and that scanner dropped and broke my right pinky toe. I remember I hit the ground and started crawling to the break table which was about 20 feet away. The lunch bell rang, and I yelled, "Tiffany!"

Tiff was my team leader and one of my best friends. We had been friends for the past two years while working at Toyota. We prayed together, did Bible study together, and we would always inform one another about our churches, when a revival was coming, and we would both go. I went to several of her church's revivals. She loved Jesus just as much as I did. We both grew in the Lord ministering to each other and sharing God's

Word with each other. Tiffany had spoken over my life so many times and I knew every time the power and anointing of God was all over it. She was a mighty woman of God and I admired her. Her faith was relentless. She stayed in the scriptures and was always studying the Word, something I really needed to work on. She was disciplined and it seemed to come easy to her.

I told her that I dropped my scanner and hurt my foot. She said, "Calm down. You're going to be okay."

I said, "No I'm not. It's my fault. I have the wrong shoes on."

I had violated safety procedures. Team members were to have all PPE on in the building. It was policy. I knew there was a strong possibility I would be terminated, and I definitely wouldn't be eligible for worker's comp.

I was just about to take vacation in two days. How could this happen? I'm hit! All I could do was pray to the Lord. I had to leave my job that day in a Toyota ambulance and I waved at my team, not knowing this would be the last time I would be working with them and I wasn't ever coming back. These people were my family. I was at Toyota for a little more than four years. It was my life. This was the longest I had ever worked anywhere. The relationships I had with the people there meant so much to me. Toyota had become a huge part of me. I felt like I was in a way defined by the job I had.

I felt like the only thing I had going for me was being able to hold a job. I put all my time and energy into making a career out of this and being the best. I was devastated.

On my way to the emergency room I knew I was going to be down for a while. All I could do was pray.

The X-rays showed that I had a fractured toe and would be on crutches for at least six weeks. I took the one week of vacation I had already put in for a couple months prior. I had room reservations in Newburgh TownePlace Suites which worked out in my favor because now I was on crutches and didn't want to go too far away. I used that time to relax and had in mind I was going to finish the book I had started that the Lord had put on my heart to write. I hung out in the pool and watched TV. I tried to write but I couldn't find the words. I just didn't feel inspired with everything that was going on. I was trying to figure out what I was going to do. SMC was going to get back with me and let me know what they were going to do with me since I was unable to even set foot in the plant with crutches.

I drove to Princeton for my second doctor's appointment after my vacation. As I was leaving, Helen from human resources called to give me the devastating news that I was terminated for violating safety procedure and not in my proper PPE. As I was driving it was raining. When I hung up the phone, I felt sick to my stomach and started bawling my eyes out. I had to pull over in the nearest parking lot. To my right, there happened to be a hotel that was no longer in business, Express Inn.

I knew this hotel had been here for years, ever since I was a little girl. I remember my mom and I stayed there one night. She and my dad were having problems. I just laid my head on the steering wheel while parked in this hotel parking lot, and I said, "Why, Lord?"

I had worked so hard. I had been terminated from almost every job I had ever worked. Is this my promotion? The Lord had promised me a promotion, and this looked nothing like it. I was shook. I felt a cloud of disappointment and despair hovering over me. I felt like a failure. I was living for God. These things aren't supposed to happen when you're living right. I had to accept the fact that I did make a mistake. It was my fault and I was the one responsible for being terminated because I broke a safety rule. But even so, Lord, You would still let this happen to me?

Then immediately He spoke and told me He had something better for me. I knew in that moment He did.

I pulled over in a parking lot that used to be a hotel. It was raining and I needed to have a breakdown. In that parking lot the Lord told me He wanted to turn it into a faith-based rehab for women and children.

I felt peace.

I called Mom and told her I was terminated. I thought she was going to be so disappointed in me. She had been so proud of me for going to work every day and having a job at Toyota. What was she going to think of me now? I felt like she was going to think the same things I was: "She lost another job? What is she going to do now?"

Mom said, "Come on over to the house so we can talk about this."

I really needed some encouragement and who other than my mother to make me feel better? I quit crying and started praising God. That's the only thing I knew to do in a desperate situation, and this was definitely one of those situations. I went to my mom's house and one of the first things I asked her was, "Are you disappointed in me, Mom?"

She said, "Nope!"

I said, "I'm kind of disappointed in myself."

She said, "Wait a minute now! I know He is doing a work in you. He has something better for you Kristin. You just hold on."

She was right. I know God is good and He has always been faithful.

I then decided to finish my GED. I had been praying fervently for Him to help me and this was the perfect opportunity for me to focus on my education. This in fact was an answered prayer. I needed the time to study and really get serious about what I was doing, so I did. I went to the library and studied almost every day, then I would go faithfully to class, where Ms. Rhonda was always encouraging me and quizzing me.

I just couldn't seem to convince myself I was smart enough. I prayed even more.

The Lord had given me so many dreams in this particular year. I believe it was in a season of divine revelation and I was finding even more of who I am in Christ Jesus. All of a sudden around June, I had Apostle Collins on my heart and I just felt like it was time for me to call him and thank him for everything I had learned and received under his ministry. The Lord had given me a dream in March that was about Louisville. I knew Apostle Collins operated in the gift of interpretation and I felt led to call him. I called him and immediately realized this was a divine appointment. I told him everything that the Lord had brought me through, and that I was experiencing dreams and visions on a regular basis.

As I told the man of God my dream, he had the interpretation, and I felt the power and anointing all over our conversation. He was so moved he was crying and completely wrecked. He was blessed and I could tell more than glad that I had overcome the drugs and homosexuality I was entangled in while under his ministry.

I was completely delivered, and my dream was confirmation of the gifts of the Spirit I found in Louisville. They were stolen but God had given them back. He said he had told his congregation many times about me, how under his ministry I had received a visitation from the Lord and he knew that I had seen the face of God and, no matter what, I would walk through. No matter how far away from God I found myself, my seeing His face was a covenant He made with me that my life would be preserved.

When I contacted him, that was that word fulfilled. My life had been preserved. I had tasted death, but the grave could not hold me. I would be resurrected just as Christ was resurrected. He then invited me to come give my testimony at his church, Miracle Life in Bowling Green, Kentucky.

I was still recovering and was getting worker's compensation. I was making just as much as I would have been making if I were still employed at Toyota, 75 percent of my wages, and I didn't have the gas expense I had commuting back and forth to Princeton. I was pretty much breaking even and was getting paid to continue my education. I was blessed and highly favored. I was so happy. I was still on crutches, but I was the happiest I had been in a long time. I was uncertain about a lot of things, but I knew if I just continued to trust God everything would fall into place.

I went to visit Apostle Collins' church and give my testimony in front of his congregation. I was treated like royalty. As soon as I touched down, I met Jasmine and Omega, two of the sweetest young ladies I had ever met. They took me out to lunch and wanted to hear all about my testimony. All they spoke of was how powerful my story was, and they were blessed that I shared that with them. These women were in an evangelistic ministry and were on fire for Jesus. They both attended Western Kentucky University to receive their bachelor's degree in different majors. These were two determined, highly intellectual black women and I was honored to hear their testimonies.

When I finally met with the apostle and first lady all I could do was cry. I had the utmost honor and respect for this man, and I loved him for the man of God he was. The first lady just loved on me and made me feel like family. I never felt so important in my entire life. They honored me and allowed me to give my testimony. I then realized this is exactly what I was supposed to be doing. I was so filled up. I knew the Lord wanted me to honor the prophet that honored God.

I thanked him for his obedience in covering me in prayer so many years ago. God used him in a mighty way and is still using him to preach the gospel and teach the five-fold ministry and the prophetic that is rarely taught in the church in this present day and time.

I remember a young lady in her early teens who came up to me and told me she also struggled with homosexuality at a young age and didn't know how to deal with it. I told her to seek God and He would see her through and will always give her a way out. I know God spoke through me to release something that she needed. It's the anointing that breaks the yoke.

I was blessed to know my struggles could help someone else overcome. I knew that the words that were spoken would be giving my testimony all over the world. I was getting a taste. Apostle Collins had a powerful prophetic word that gave me confirmation that I would not struggle doing His work.

God had given a vision when I was on my way back from my doctor's appointment in Princeton, and every time I would turn that curve right there by the softball fields I played in as a child, the Holy Spirit would speak to me about the Express Inn Hotel that was vacant. He gave me a God-idea. That hotel would soon be a rehabilitation center for women and children who have struggled with addiction. It would be run like the rehab in Louisville I was in at Wayside.

I pulled in the Express Inn and saw a for sale sign. I immediately knew this was a sign from the Lord. I called the number that was on the sign. It was an Indian lady who owned the property. I asked her how much the property was, and she asked me what I planned to do with it. I told her the Lord had put on my heart to turn that hotel into a rehab for women and children. She said she had prayed for the Lord to give her a sign that morning and then I called. She had been off of work and the business was no longer running due to her being injured. I told her that I had lost my job at Toyota due to my injury. She then explained to me how she had always wanted to turn the Express Inn into a place to help homeless and women who have suffered from addictions and domestic violence.

I knew in that moment this was God and He would make a way in His perfect timing to make this happen. I was driving down Highway 41 on my way back home to Evansville while having this conversation with "Pretty," the lady who owned this hotel. All of a sudden I felt the unction to meet with her. At that moment, I was hit by the power of God and felt the anointing all over this phone call. We met at McDonald's in Princeton for lunch. I had coffee and she ate lunch and we just talked about the things of God and all the things He had brought us through. A lot of the trials and tribulations we both faced were in total darkness and we had both acknowledged the power of Jesus Christ who brought us through.

She asked me how I was going to get the money to buy this hotel and I said, "The Lord is going to give it to me." She gave me a look as if she was a little unsure, but it was my faith that gave me this assurance. I told her, "When the Lord blesses me with the provisions and resources, I'm going to need to purchase this hotel."

I told her I would get in touch with her and she was thrilled with the idea.

After fully recovering from my injury, I was in a quiet season. Everything was really still for me. After my worker's comp depleted, the Lord blessed me to be able to receive unemployment benefits to carry me through the rest of the year. The Lord always made a way for all of my bills to be paid and plenty of food to eat. I never wanted for anything. I had always had everything I needed even while I was unemployed.

I was preparing and studying to take my GED test before Christmas. I took math, language, reading, science, and a writing essay. By the grace of God, I found out the second week of January that I had passed all but math. I was still looking for a job. With all the ones I applied for everything fell through. I felt like it was because I didn't have my GED. I felt a lot of pressure and was feeling defeated. I was determined to keep going and I wasn't giving up.

I went to my Christmas party and met the CEO of Catanese Realty Professionals with Keller Williams and I was hired on the spot. I started the new year with a full-time office job with a beautiful view from the third floor of German American Bank — another prayer the Lord has answered for me. I was also blessed to attend Family Reunion in Dallas for training. What a blessing! I always wanted a job where I was able to travel and here it was! When I was looking over downtown Dallas, I knew without a doubt I was right where God told me He was taking me to, a room full of millionaires and billionaires, and this was where I belonged. It wasn't the money. It was the honor He had brought me to, a place in Him I never knew existed.

I studied geometry and algebra all the way up until March 3, 2020. I took my math test that day and passed. March 3 is a marker day for me. Something about the

3rd day of the 3rd month is significant for me. The 3rd day of the 3rd month 2015, the Lord brought me back home and His hand has been over my life ever since.

This 2020 has been a remarkable year. I have walked into the promotion God had spoken to me; I received my GED I'd been praying for and have waited 22 years to get; I look at all of the prayers that have been answered, all of the lost that I have been blessed to minister to who have come to Jesus and are experiencing the goodness of God and have been brought out of darkness; the blessings that I have received and the truth that has been revealed in my life — the best is still yet to come!

In the name of Jesus, the plan and purpose God has for me will be fulfilled, and all the glory is given to my Savior and Lord, Jesus Christ.

I'm in a place of refreshing rain!

Unless we have showers, our hearts will get hard.

Have you ever seen rain fall when the ground was so hard that the water didn't soak in? Picture people coming to church when the Spirit is moving and the rain of His presence rolls off, like water from a duck's back, because their hearts are too hard to receive it.

The rain of the Spirit brings repentance and will break the soil of the shallow and hard ground of our heart. This latter rain of refreshing allows us to produce more and more fruit.

23

CHAPTER 23

He Called My Name

In 2012 God called me by name. He had been preparing me internally for visitation. I was diligently seeking Him but overwhelmed in sin and looking for a way out. He met me right where I was. He came in the darkness with me not to leave me there but to bring me out. He is truly the light in the darkness. He brought me to a place to soften my heart, a safe place to where I would be able to receive his invitation to the things of God. A visitation with Jesus: Who can be prepared for something like that?

God, who is all knowing, knew I wasn't prepared for deliverance. He knew my heart had to be cultivated for visitation from Him. He knew I was going to fall and was going to taste death, and He knew I would be resurrected by His Spirit. Genesis 32:30 (NIV) says, *"So Jacob called the place Peniel, saying, 'It is because I saw God face to face, and yet my life was spared.'"*

God knew He was going to make a covenant with me. Battling addiction for 16 years, the Lord knew I had the victory. He knew the end of my story was not defeat. He knew I would overcome. I would eventually in life find my true identity in Him.

God's love never supersedes His holiness, and no matter what darkness and sin I may get myself into, His love will never run out. He will be there in the upcoming years and seasons to meet me right where I am and to bring me out in His perfect timing. It was not a coincidence that I was under an apostolic ministry to prepare me for His face-to-face visitation. The mercy of God will always be with me, and His grace. Even when I make my bed in hell and am cast into outer darkness, He came to save me. Death could not ever hold me. His covenant is through eternity. He would soon snatch me out of darkness for His purpose and His glory. God is everlasting to everlasting. The Bible says Jesus has the keys to death.

Even when I felt hopelessness to the extreme of seeing no way out, He was there.

There is only one way, and that way is Jesus.

In a season of blessings with an open heaven, I see door after door being opened. Doors that had been shut for me are now opened. The Lord gave my spiritual dad, Apostle Chad, a man of God appointed to me for the seasons to come, a key to unlock a door that had been shut. The anointing that this man of God carries was needed for me to move forward in my walk. The words that were spoken carried power. Doors flew open within seventy-two hours of being spoken. A true prophet's words will not be empty. The power of the spoken word is intended to come out of the mouth of a prophet.

Now, being in a prosperous place in life, being strong in the Lord and knowing without a shadow of doubt who I am in Christ and the Freedom I walk in, it allows me to have a completely different perspective on life. I'm not looking back to the things I was caught up in in the world, but I'm looking forward with a new set of eyes. Before, I could not see the road ahead of me, the goodness and the grace of God. I was unable to perceive the things of God because I was in darkness. Tasting some of the deeper things of the Spirit, like dreams and visions, I can see the kingdom of God that is near. When I was called before the foundations of the earth were formed, He knew me. He knew He was going to train me to be a Mighty Princess Warrior of God. He saw already what He had purposed for me to walk in. During my darkest moments He knew me. The person I am now can never be compared to the person I once was. I am a new creature in Christ, the old made new. I have dreams and visions of where I want to see myself in the future and I believe that God will give me the desires of my heart. I never thought I would see myself where I am today. Looking back, I thank God my yesterday is gone.

The only way you can walk in the things God has purposed for you to walk in is if He allows your eyes to be opened, the scales to fall off. The Bible declares in Psalm 119:18 (KJV), *"Open thou mine eyes, that I may behold wondrous things out of thy law."*

He removed the veil from the eyes of my heart — my understanding. There is a veil of darkness and ignorance on the hearts of all men, with respect to divine and spiritual things. Their understandings are darkened — with darkness itself. To see the true light, this veil must be removed, the scales must drop, and eyes must be opened and enlightened, just as the psalmist here petitions, and the apostle prays for the Ephesians:

"I pray that the eyes of your heart may be enlightened in order that you may know the hope to which he has called you, the riches of his glorious inheritance" (Ephesians 1:18, NIV).

When scales fall from your eyes, you suddenly realize the truth. When the eyes of your understanding are opened to God's wisdom, you realize you were walking through deception. Not having wisdom and understanding is to be spiritual blindness. The Spirit of the Lord is the resurrection power that allows you to see and receive revelation. *Though it cost all you have, get understanding* (Proverbs 4:7, NIV). *The one who cherishes understanding will soon prosper* (Proverbs 19:8, NIV).

As I am introduced to the things of the Spirit, being taught, and going through seasons of discipleship, my teaching is through the Holy Spirit. God himself speaks to me through dreams and, when I am ready, He will give me revelation of the dreams He has given me. I feel as if something has been activated in the earth — in me, in my heart. I have had the want and desire to educate myself about dreams and dream interpretation. The Lord has clearly put that desire in my heart. I believe it has everything to do with my gifting and what God has called me to do. I have been praying for the Lord to give me wisdom and understanding. I believe He is giving me just that. He is answering my prayers and teaching me by His Spirit. Walking with the Lord and walking in the Spirit is an honor. My heart's desire is to live a continuous lifestyle of being led by His Spirit.

THE END FROM THE BEGINNING

24

CHAPTER 24

Through The Storm

On August 5, 2020, I tested positive for COVID-19. I was shocked! How could a child of God who is faithful and on fire for Jesus catch this? I believed that if it came near me it would die because the power of God and the fire of God is all over me.

Psalm 91 (NIV) declares, *"Whoever dwells in the shelter of the Most High will rest in the shadow of the Almighty. I will say of the Lord, 'He is my refuge and my fortress, my God, in whom I will trust.' Surely He will save you from the fowler's snare and from the deadly pestilence. He will cover you with his feathers, and under his wings you will find refuge; his faithfulness will be your shield and rampart. You will not fear the terror of night, nor the arrow that flies by day, nor the pestilence that stalks in the darkness, nor the plague that destroys at midday. A thousand may fall at your side, ten thousand at your right hand, but it will not come near you. You will only observe with your eyes and see the punishment of the wicked. If you say, 'The Lord is my refuge,' and you make the Most High your dwelling, no harm will overtake you, no disaster will come near your tent. For he will command his angels concerning you to guard you in all your ways; they will lift you up in their hands, so that you will not strike your foot against a stone. You will tread on the lion and the cobra; you will trample the great lion and the serpent. 'Because he loves me,' says the Lord, 'I will rescue him; I will protect him, for he acknowledges my name. He will call on me, and I will answer him; I will be with him in trouble, I will deliver him and honor him. With long life I will satisfy him and show him my salvation.'"*

So why would a faithful daughter of the king have to experience COVID-19? The Lord will always test your faith. In order for us to go from glory to glory and faith to faith we must face trials and tribulations. We must walk through darkness walking by faith not by sight, to finally see the light.

I am not the same woman that walked into that storm. I am stronger and wiser. Every battle that we face takes us from glory to glory and faith to faith as long as we never give up and always keep moving forward.

Thank you, Jesus!

"And once the storm is over,

you won't remember how you made it through,

how you managed to survive.

You won't even be sure,

whether the storm is really over.

But one thing is certain.

When you come out of the storm,

you won't be the same person who walked in.

That's what this storm's all about."

— Haruki Murkami, *Kafka on the Shore*

"Do not let anyone work harder than you. In the end some of your greatest pains become your greatest strengths."

- Kristin Hardiman

**To contact the author,
or to request additional copies
of this book ($14.95/each), write:**

Kristin Hardiman

P.O. Box 2046

Evansville IN 47728

or email

KristinHardiman9@gmail.com

Make your check or money order payable to Kristin Hardiman
or send PayPal funds to KristinHardiman9@gmail.com

Made in the USA
Columbia, SC
20 September 2020